Southern Living.

1999 Garden ANNUAL

A pathway of mahonia, Lenten roses,
Jet Trail quince, and Japanese black
pine (See pages 40–43.)

Southern Living®

1999 Garden ANNUAL

Oxmoor House®

Southern Living.
1999 Garden ANNUAL

©1999 by Oxmoor House, Inc.
Book Division of Southern Progress Corporation
P.O. Box 2463, Birmingham, Alabama 35201

Southern Living® is a federally registered
trademark of Southern Living, Inc.

ISSN: 1048-2318
Hardcover ISBN: 0-8487-1824-0
Softcover ISBN: 0-8487-1826-7
Manufactured in the United States of America
First Printing 1999

SOUTHERN LIVING
Garden Editor: Linda C. Askey
Senior Writer: Stephen P. Bender
Senior Photographers: Van Chaplin, Allen Rokach
Photographers: Jean M. Allsopp, Tina Cornett
Assistant Garden Design Editor: Rebecca Bull Reed
Assistant Garden Editors: Ellen Riley, Charles Thigpen
Homes Editor: Julia Hamilton Thomason
Production Manager: Kenner Patton
Assistant Production Manager: Bradford Kachelhofer
Editorial Assistant: Lynne Long

OXMOOR HOUSE, INC.
Editor-in-Chief: Nancy Fitzpatrick Wyatt
Editorial Director, Special Interest Publications:
Ann H. Harvey
Senior Editor, Editorial Services: Olivia Kindig Wells
Art Director: James Boone

1999 SOUTHERN LIVING GARDEN ANNUAL
Editor: Kelly Hooper Troiano
Copy Editor: Cathy Ritter Scholl
Designer: Carol Loria
Editorial Assistant: Heather Averett
Indexer: Katharine R. Wiencke

Director, Production and Distribution: Phillip Lee
Associate Production Manager: Vanessa C. Richardson
Production Assistant: Faye Porter Bonner

We're Here for You!
We at Oxmoor House are dedicated to serving you with reliable
information that expands your imagination and enriches your life.
We welcome your comments and
suggestions. Please write us at:

OXMOOR HOUSE, INC.
Editor, *1999 Southern Living Garden Annual*
2100 Lakeshore Drive
Birmingham, AL 35209

Cover: *Oriental hybrid lilies*
Back Cover: *Trumpet vine and azaleas*

Contents

Larkspur

Lenten rose

Chrysanthemums

Red cedar

*H*olding an entire year in the garden in your hand is not unusual. You do it every time you pick up a seed or plant catalog. But what you are holding at the moment is not the promise of a year to come, but a year fulfilled—the collected gardening articles of *Southern Living* from 1998.

From the earliest blooms that break as winter breathes its last chilly breath to autumn's fire and the holiday's warmth, you can take an armchair stroll through the garden year and consider the possibilities for your own plantings.

On these pages we take you on visits to homes and gardens across the South. Enjoy yourself, and borrow inspiration from these neighbors. Just as they welcomed our writers and photographers into their gardens, they share their joy of gardening with you.

Likewise, we feel that the only thing that's better than visiting gardens around the South is coming home to spend a day in our own. We hope you find the same pleasure as you turn the page and look back on a year that bloomed.

Linda C. Askey
Garden Editor

A boxwood-lined path leads from a renovated porch into a small garden.
(See pages 34–35.)

Common camellia and azaleas (See pages 18–19.)

January

Checklist
for
January

EDITORS' NOTEBOOK
It has golden flowers, arching stems, and blooms in late winter. What is it? If you answered "forsythia," then you ought to be ashamed. Haven't you been faithfully reading your Royal Horticultural Society Encyclopedia every night before bed? Then you should recognize winter jasmine *(Jasminum nudiflorum)*. It grows just about everywhere and starts blooming with the year's first hint of mild weather, often in January, and continuing through February. This adaptable cascading shrub is a great choice for planting atop a retaining wall or steep bank. And its bright green stems make it look like an evergreen— a trait every Southern gardener holds dear. So tonight, as you reverently study your encyclopedia, pay special attention to winter jasmine. There'll be a pop quiz in the morning.

Steve Bender

A little effort each month will keep your garden looking its best all season long. You'll find a checklist at the beginning of each chapter with suggestions of what to do that month.

TIPS

☐ **Bed prep**—Use this time to turn under fall leaves or compost or add lime and other amendments to your soil. Remember, if your soil is too wet, you could do more harm than good. Wait until it crumbles easily in your hand.

☐ **Camellias**—Lower and Coastal South gardeners should select shrubs thoughtfully to enjoy their blooms through the winter months. Early ones include Debutante and Professor Sargent, followed by midseason selections such as Brilliant and Empress. Rev. John G. Drayton and Governor Mouton bloom later, extending the season into March.

☐ **Plan first**—Plant on paper before you go to the garden. Moving things around is easier with an eraser than a spade. Graph paper and a 50-foot tape measure will help you get your house, your lot, and your bed drawn to the correct scale. Then use tracing paper positioned on top of your graph paper to sketch your ideas. Just use a fresh sheet for each new version.

☐ **Poinsettias**—For long-lasting color, select plants with large, fully colored bracts (colored leaves) and little green buttons at the center. Each button is a flower, and it should be intact and beginning to open. Maintain your plant by keeping it between 55 and 70 degrees; out of drafts; and in bright, indirect light for about six hours each day. Do not allow the plant to wilt or the soil to become soggy in foil wrap.

☐ **Vegetables**—Continue harvesting collards and kale. These vegetables are sweetened by the cold weather. Cut only the lowest leaves, leaving the top portion of each stalk intact to continue growing.

PLANT

☐ **Annuals**—This is a good time to set out transplants of cool-weather annuals in the Lower South. Good choices include pansies, sweet William, calendulas, and pinks. Wait until late next month in the Middle South. ▶

☐ **Fruit**—Plant deciduous fruit such as blueberries, grapes, raspberries, pears, or figs right away in the Lower and Coastal South so they can grow roots before spring. When buying bare-root trees, be sure that the roots are packed in a moist material or that the trees are containerized.

☐ **Ground covers**—Plant ground covers now in the Middle, Lower, and Coastal South. Amend the entire bed by tilling in 4 inches of organic matter such as compost, as well as a controlled-release fertilizer such as 12-6-6 according to label directions. Keep the planting well watered during the dry winter months.

☐ **Perennials**—In the Lower and Coastal South plant yarrow, oxeye and Shasta daisies, gaillardia, coreopsis, and purple coneflowers now for color in the spring and summer. For maximum impact in the garden, plant each type in a mass of a single color.

◀ **Primulas**—Festive pots of primulas brighten your home in winter with pink, red, yellow, orange, and purple flowers. In the Lower South plant them in beds outdoors.

◄ **Roses**—In Florida, plant bare-root roses in a well-drained, sunny spot. Soak the roots in a bucket of water for a couple of hours before planting. Roses grafted on Fortuniana rootstock live longest. You can also plant container-grown roses at this time. Select from fragrant antique roses such as Souvenir de la Malmaison and Paul Neyron or modern favorites such as Tropicana, Queen Elizabeth, and Dortmund.

☐ **Seeds**—Select a sunny window or greenhouse to start seeds of sweet alyssum, petunias, calendulas, and ornamental cabbage and kale for later transplanting in the garden or into containers.

☐ **Transplant**—Deciduous and evergreen shrubs and trees may be easily moved with little transplant shock from now through early March. Be sure to water well at planting to settle soil around the roots. Stake trees to reduce damage from winter winds.

☐ **Vegetables**—In the Lower South plant potatoes, mustard greens, turnips, carrots, cauliflower, and broccoli now for a spring harvest.

PRUNE

☐ **Cold damage**—Should frost nip back bananas or other tender plants in Coastal South gardens, leave them alone until spring. The browned tops will help shelter the plants from future cold. In spring, you can remove dead leaves or stems. Watch new growth on hibiscus and other woody shrubs; prune to direct them as needed.

☐ **Dianthus**—Lower and Coastal South gardeners will find that annual dianthus such as the Telstar hybrids have a surprising resistance to heat. Planted in a well-drained, sunny spot, they may last into summer. Snip off the old blossoms and tips of stems from any dianthus, including sweet William, that was planted last fall. Fertilize with a controlled-release fertilizer such as 18-18-18.

☐ **Flowerbeds**—Don't be tempted to clean up your perennial beds too early. Let the browned tops remain. They catch and hold fall leaves that will insulate the crowns of your plants.

☐ **Fruit trees and grapes**—These plants are dormant and most benefit from pruning and fertilizing now. Peaches live longer and produce more if pruned each year. Form an open center so that light can reach the ripening fruit.

☐ **Thin crepe myrtles**—Remove twiggy growth and limbs that cross or touch one another to expose the beautiful sculptural quality of crepe myrtle trunks. You can train them for single or multiple trunks. Either way, remove excess suckers from the base of the tree. ►

CONTROL

☐ **Pest control**—To beat mites, whiteflies, and scale, spray pest-prone plants such as gardenias and camellias with horticultural oil when the temperature is between 40° and 85°F.

WINTER SCENTS

The earthy scent of idle soil and decaying leaves gives way to subtle, sweet drifts of winter flowers. A sprinkle of warm days in January is just enough to make swelled buds unfurl, releasing breaths of perfume and life into the garden.

Each year across the South January proves to be a fickle month. A few teasing, warm, sunny days can be followed by a cold arctic blast. Remember to appreciate the warm days because with them come winter flowers. This is a season in limbo, when beautiful blooms can be killed in a single night's hard freeze. If cold weather is predicted while your flowers are blooming, simply cut a fistful and bring them inside. This way you can enjoy them a little longer.

Here are a few plants that brighten the winter landscape and scent a room.

Wintersweet *(Chimonanthus praecox)* has small, waxy, yellow blooms. The flowers aren't showy but are perfumed. This large, slow-growing deciduous shrub can reach 12 to 15 feet. Wintersweet thrives in full sun to partial shade.

Winter daphne *(Daphne odora)* is a small mounded evergreen shrub with slick, glossy leaves. It rarely grows over 3 feet high. Small clusters of compact white or pink blooms appear in January. Winter daphne can be finicky to grow but its good looks make it a worthy winter specimen. Dappled shade, light waterings, and well-drained soil will keep this shrub happy.

Witch hazel *(Hamamelis vernalis, H. mollis,* and

H. x *intermedia)* blooms have yellow, orange, or reddish ribbonlike petals, depending on the selection. What the flowers lack in show they make up for in spicy, sweet scent. This large deciduous shrub or small tree can grow 15 to 20 feet in height. Witch hazels prefer filtered light and work well in a woodland setting.

Winter honeysuckle *(Lonicera fragrantissima)* is a large, deciduous, mounding shrub that can grow 10 to 15 feet in height and width. Cream-colored flowers line the branches and smell lemony and sweet. It's not a fussy plant and will grow in sun or shade.

Star magnolia *(Magnolia stellata)* can be a deciduous small tree or a large shrub, growing slowly to 15 to 20 feet in height. Fuzzy brown buds pop open in late winter producing multipetaled white to faint pink, sweet-smelling flowers. It thrives in full sun to partial shade and performs best in fertile, well-drained soil.

Japanese flowering apricot *(Prunus mume)* is a small tree rarely seen in gardens, but it's worth looking for. Depending on the selection it has white-, pink-, to rose-colored petals with showy yellow stamens. Plant as you would a dogwood.

Paperwhites *(Narcissus tazetta)* can be enjoyed all winter and into spring. In the fall, pot up a few bulbs; then wait a few weeks and pot up more. Staggered plantings are easy to care for and can reward you with the strong-scented paperwhites.

Some common **pansies** when planted in masses can produce a blanket of fragrance. Yellow pansies of the Crystal Bowl series are especially strong scented and cold-weather tolerant. Pansies can bloom sporadically throughout the winter and will peak in the spring. ◇

(For sources see pages 250–251.)

(Left to right) *winter honeysuckle, paperwhites, winter daphne, witch hazel, Crystal Bowl pansies, star magnolia, wintersweet, Japanese flowering apricot*

BY CHARLIE THIGPEN ■ PHOTOGRAPHY JEAN ALLSOPP

Plants can be as striking as any sculpture and are far more affordable.

the art of
houseplants

Elevate simple houseplants from an afterthought to a work of art—nature's art. If they are corralled in a pool of sunlight by the windowsill, their possibilities may never be realized. But when singled out and properly presented, a houseplant makes a visual statement. For in the right setting, the distinctive shape and texture of a foliage plant lends character and drama to a room, just like a painting or sculpture would.

Begin by selecting the right one. When choosing a plant, keep in mind that it should have simple lines. If you want a look that is light and airy, select a houseplant that gives you that impression, such as the feathery foliage of a palm. For a bold stroke, choose one that has big leaves, such as a

(Above) *This Chinese fan palm has a simple, repetitive form that dominates the more intricate patterns around it.*

(Left) *With the character of molded clay, the aged trunk of a ponytail palm echoes the exaggerated figure of the artwork.*

BY LINDA C. ASKEY ■ PHOTOGRAPHY VAN CHAPLIN

(Above) *Even the most common of plants can have presence. Algerian ivy cascades from a tall pedestal, anchoring the corner of the room.*

(Left) *Atop a pedestal, this large pot of mixed bromeliads assumes a position that's usually reserved for sculpture.*

bird-of-paradise or a bromeliad. Plants with many small leaves and branches—such as a ficus tree—are difficult to use in this way.

For quick impact, elevate your plant on a pedestal. Most of us are unaccustomed to looking up at a bromeliad, so a pedestal gives you a fresh perspective and a new appreciation for the plant. Besides, smaller plants are typically less expensive, and you can have the presence of an indoor tree with a tabletop model if you stage it right.

Of course, not all plants will thrive on a pedestal in a dimly lit room. If the location is not ideal for the growth of the plant, keep two that look good in that location and rotate them every week or so. By using two different types of plants, you are less likely to tire of the arrangement.

Lighting gives drama to the theater, and it will also work in your home. Shining a light up or down on a plant, or aiming a small, inconspicuous spotlight to wash across it to create shadows of the branches on the walls, multiplies the effect. ◇

OTHER
SCULPTURAL
CHOICES

split-leaf
philodendron

Black Cardinal
philodendron

fishtail palm

corn plant

most dracaenas

Easy Arrangements

An arrangement does not have to consist of perishable cut flowers. The many small foliage plants you find at local plant shops and garden centers may be all the material you need to fashion a centerpiece that is colorful and long lasting. Karin Purvis, owner of The Houseplant in Greenville, South Carolina, designed two arrangements using a single type of plant in each one.

Rex begonias are some of the most colorful foliage plants, so they are ready replacements for fresh flowers. Karin's begonia basket is low and broad, ideal for showcasing the diversity of leaf shapes and patterns available. Rather than having individual pots to water, she lined this basket with plastic, took plants out of their containers, set them in the basket, and filled the space between them with potting soil.

Because they are planted, these begonias will actually grow in this setting. The key is to water enough to keep the plants healthy but not so much that they drown. Remember, there is no drainage for excess water. If you have any doubt about watering, stick your finger in the soil or pick up the basket to see how heavy it is.

If watered carefully, this planter will last until the plants become overcrowded or you tire of them. However, Karin cautions that some sun is required to maintain the brilliant leaf color. Perhaps you have another arrangement of foliage that you can alternate, moving one to a sunny window to get recharged.

A bowl of flaming sword bromeliads (*Vriesea splendens* Major) makes a striking centerpiece, and it couldn't be simpler to reproduce. Five pots rest on each other in the bowl, angling their flamelike flowers outward. The best part is that it will last for months.

Even after the flowers fade—which will take several weeks—you can clip them off and enjoy the old as well as the new emerging foliage. To maintain the centerpiece, Karin takes the plants (still in the bowl) to the sink and sprays the entire arrangement; she then tips the bowl to drain the excess water.

Linda C. Askey

Five flaming sword bromeliads and a pottery bowl are just about all it takes to make this colorful centerpiece.

Line a basket with plastic and fill it with potting soil. Because there are no drainage holes, no moisture leaks onto your furniture, but you could kill the plants by overwatering them.

The Well-Placed
CAMELLIA

BY STEVE BENDER

PHOTOGRAPHY VAN CHAPLIN, SYLVIA MARTIN

Like many of you, I get a kick out of discovering rarities. A Gutenberg Bible signed by Gutie himself. A 3-year-old who refuses to whine. A common camellia well placed in the garden.

Of these, the well-placed camellia is of course the rarest. Why that is, I don't know. Somewhere way back in the annals of English common law must be written the following statement: "Garden camellias shall be so located as to obscure windows, block easy entrance to the house, and require exhaustive pruning every fourth day." Southerners, being law-abiding folks, naturally took this decree to heart.

Thus, our principal sin regarding common camellias is failing to plan for their mature size. We plant them as if they were azaleas or rhododendrons. But these bushy, rounded evergreens often reach 15 to 25 feet high.

"People just don't realize that their cute, little camellia is going to grow," observes Charlotte landscape architect Brian Zimmerman. "It takes foresight to look down the road 5, 10, 15 years from now and see what that puppy wants to do. So when we do a plan for someone, we always explain what the mature size will be. And we position camellias so that they can attain full size without being butchered every year."

What's a good spot for a common camellia? Definitely not beneath a window or next to a door. If you insist on having one close to the house, place it on a corner or against a large, bare wall. Away from the house, try it in a wood-

Semidouble flowers, such as Ville de Nantes, are less freeze-prone than doubles.

land garden, courtyard garden, beneath some tall shade trees, or at the rear of a shrub border.

Nashville landscape architect Ben Page thinks of camellias as evergreens first and flowering plants second. "They are very elegant shrubs," he says. "Use them as you would a Nellie R. Stevens or Burford holly, where you need a big, structural plant for a deep green background. Camellias have such interesting, variable leaves—some are small and refined, others are great big. They make wonderful foils for other plants with different textures and leaf colors. The flowers are almost incidental."

Common camellias have been popular Southern plants ever since seedsman David Landreth started distributing them from his Charleston, South Carolina, store around 1818. But they won't do just anywhere. In *Azaleas and Camellias,* published in 1946, author H. Harold Hume writes, "Roughly, the area in which the camellia can be grown . . . corresponds to that in which climatic conditions are suitable for the growing of cotton." For those of you whose chief knowledge of cotton comes from fondling a flannel shirt, let me be more specific.

The first limiting factor of common camellias is winter cold. Although most survive brief bouts with frigid 5- to 10-degree air, their flowers and flowerbuds don't. Thus, gardeners in the Upper South and parts of the Middle South should either grow them in containers they can bring indoors for winter or plant them in protected courtyards.

Camellias grace winter and spring with single, semidouble, or double blossoms in colors ranging from deep red to white.

The second limitation is soil. Camellias need moist, acid soil (pH 5.5 to 6.5) rich in organic matter. Clay, gumbo, and other heavy soils must be avoided. Camellias want perfect drainage. They don't want wet feet. That's why experts recommend planting a camellia so that the top of the root ball is 1 inch above the soil surface. Then mulch thoroughly. If your soil is soggy, plant camellias in a raised bed.

Camellias prefer full or partial shade. The larger a camellia's leaves, the more shade it likes. Shade is especially important in winter. "If the plant has a sunny, southern exposure, the constant fluctuation of being warmed during the day and chilled at night will dehydrate it," notes Brian. A shady, northern exposure is best. An eastern one is okay, too, as long as the morning's first sun doesn't strike the plant and thaw the buds too rapidly.

If your area is prone to sudden cold snaps in winter try semidouble flowering selections, such as Berenice Boddy and Lady van Sittart, instead of big doubles. Semidouble blossoms open quickly, so they are less likely to be frozen halfway developed.

Should this shrub strike your fancy, you can find sources on pages 250–251. We will, of course, require you to promise that you won't plant them in front of your windows. ◇

Plant common camellias at the rear of shrub borders so you won't have to constantly prune them.

A Personal Appeal From
LENTEN ROSE

One of the finest ground covers for shade, Lenten rose combines handsome evergreen foliage with lovely, late-winter flowers.

WANTED—Attractive, easy-to-grow perennial. Must be shade-loving and evergreen. Showy flowers a definite plus. If you have what it takes, respond in writing to Heart & Soil.

Dear Heart & Soil,

Your prayers have been answered. Allow me to introduce myself. My name is Lenten rose *(Helleborus orientalis)*. And if I do say so myself, I'm everything you could ever want in a perennial.

Attractive? Just take a look at the enclosed snapshots. My leathery, evergreen leaves radiate from a central point, just like the fingers of your hand. They stand about 8 inches tall and blend well with ferns, hostas, and other shade-loving plants. Forming a loosely woven blanket covering the ground, they permit spring bulbs to come up through them, if that's what you want.

Showy flowers? You've hit the jackpot. I stay in bloom for six weeks or more. Nodding blossoms first appear around Valentine's Day in the Lower South and about a month later in the Upper South. White is the dominant color, but for every three plants with white flowers, you'll find one with rose blossoms. Either color makes a long-lasting cut flower. Just place the stems in water.

Easy to grow? That's me all over. The only places I refuse to grow are the Coastal and Tropical South. I like moist, fertile, well-drained soil that contains lots of organic matter. If the soil is too acid (pH 6.0 or lower), sprinkle a little lime over the soil surface once a year. While you're at it, sprinkle some slow-release fertilizer, such as Osmocote 14-14-14 too. Shade is a must, especially in the hot afternoon.

Frankly, yours truly is about the best investment you could make. I'm easy to propagate. Just divide established plants in fall or spring. Or transplant the many seedlings that sprout in spring.

Well, I've made my case. I anxiously await your response. ◇

(For sources see pages 250–251.)

AT A GLANCE

Size: 6 to 8 inches; 10 to 14 inches with flowers

Light: shade, especially in the afternoon

Soil: moist, fertile, well drained

Propagation: seed, division

Range: Upper, Middle, Lower South

Expect to pay: $5 to $10 per plant

BY STEVE BENDER ■ PHOTOGRAPHY VAN CHAPLIN

I Can't Believe I Get All These Catalogs

Dr. Sigmund Freud
Oedipal Post-Life Institute
Suite 10D
The Great Beyond

Dear Dr. Freud:

Sorry to disturb your eternal rest, but my anxiety is overwhelming. I don't go out anymore. I don't receive visitors. The thought of opening my front door fills me with dread. They're out there waiting for me. They never stop coming. The catalogs—gardening catalogs.

It all began years ago on a cold, dark January day. I was sitting alone in my living room, bored, listless, needing a diversion. Suddenly, something slipped through the mail slot— a catalog, filled with wondrous plants and flowers from all over the world. My joy was overpowering. I pored over its pages, examining every photograph, recording each word. Every molecule of my body coveted those plants. And then, Dr. Freud, I made a fatal mistake, however. I placed an order. I did!

The plants came, but something else came too. Another catalog. Then another. And another! Somehow, the first catalog had transmitted my name to all the other catalogs. I bought a mailbox to handle the overflow. Then a garden cart. But it was like using a thimble to empty the ocean.

At first, I maintained a positive attitude. All these catalogs meant someone was interested in me. They only wanted to help me. There was a catalog for every kind of plant I could want. I had catalogs for seeds, perennials, trees, and bulbs. I had catalogs for fruit, herbs, and vegetables. It was like belonging to the Catalog of the Month Club—only instead of receiving one every 30 days, I received 30 every day.

I learned some important lessons about ordering, Sigmund (may I call you Sigmund?). First, always check the guarantee policy. Some catalogs guarantee their plants for a full year. Others only guarantee that plants will arrive alive. If a catalog won't guarantee dormant plants to leaf out in spring, don't order.

I learned to check shipping dates too. Mail-order nurseries in the North, I discovered, often can't ship outdoor plants between December and March because they're under snow. Southern nurseries have no such constraints. The best nurseries in either region will ship plants at a good time for planting in your area.

What else did I discover? Not to blindly order on the basis of price. You don't get something for nothing, Sigmund. When someone offers a 5-foot tree for $1.29, it probably means roots are extra. I also shy away from catalogs that mislabel plants (e.g., liatris labeled as lythrum), offer things too good to

STEVE'S TOP FIVE

Here are some not-so-common catalogs you'll appreciate.

- **The Crownsville Nursery,** (410) 849-3143; free. Superb selection of perennials and shrubs.
- **Fairweather Gardens,** (609) 451-6261; $3. Chock-full of rare beauties.
- **Forestfarm,** (541) 846-7269; $4. If you can't find it here, you probably can't find it.
- **Gardener's Supply Company,** 1-800-863-1700; free. Best mail-order source for tools and supplies.
- **Johnny's Selected Seeds,** (207) 437-4301; free. Wonderful selection of vegetable seed.

be true ("Impressionist's Garden— In a Can!"), or doctor photographs. (The only truly blue roses are the phony ones painted on a catalog's cover.)

Most worthwhile catalogs include cultural information alongside their plants, telling you whether they like sun or shade, wet or dry soil, how hardy they are, and so on. Unfortunately, Sigmund, many Northern catalogs will tell you how cold-hardy a plant is, but don't have the foggiest notion of how heat-tolerant it is. Thus, they'll say delphiniums are perennial, even though our Southern heat and humidity kills them inside of a year. So I'd suggest checking with experienced local gardeners before ordering some exotic plant you've never grown.

My house just shook! Another catalog delivery. If I open the door, they'll flood in like a wave. Drowning in paper has always been my greatest fear.

I know what to do. I'm grinding up these catalogs, Sigmund, into a fine compost to mix with soil. They'll never see the light of another day. Into the soil they go. So long! Farewell! Auf wiedersehen! Goodbye!

What? Something's coming up out of the pot! A catalog seedling! And another! Get away from me, you postal parasites, you direct-mail demons, you bulk-rate barbarians! Get away!

They've filled the room. I can't breathe. Help me, Sigmund! Help m— *Steve Bender*

Parking Court Scores

A parking area is for parking cars. It's supposed to be practical, not pretty, right? Not so, according to St. Petersburg landscape architect Phil Graham. He designed a parking court that is so good-looking, it seems a crime to park cars on it.

Key to this particular design are wire-cut bricks laid in a basket-weave pattern atop a concrete slab. The scoring of their upper surface catches light, emphasizing the checkerboard effect. It also gives the bricks a wonderfully rich texture. Despite their sophisticated look, wire-cut bricks generally cost no more than ordinary ones.

If you look closely, you'll notice that the bricks aren't mortared. They're butted together and glued to the slab.

No mortar was used—the bricks were butted together and glued to the slab. Laying them this way requires full-size 4- x 8-inch brick pavers.

A concrete apron framing the parking court helps the adhesive keep them in place. Laying bricks this way requires full-size 4- x 8-inch bricks. It won't work with the slightly smaller ones that are commonly used with mortar.

To appreciate another noteworthy aspect, you'll have to walk across the street. See how the island of palms in front of the parking court separates it from the street? The trunks and fronds hide just enough of the house and parking to create a sense of intimacy.

As this example demonstrates, even the most utilitarian areas needn't be dull. Attention to detail can turn the truly mundane into a work of art.

Steve Bender

(Above) *The bricks were laid in a basket-weave pattern atop a concrete slab.*

(Inset) *Palms and other trees screen just enough of the parking court to give it a sense of enclosure and intimacy.*

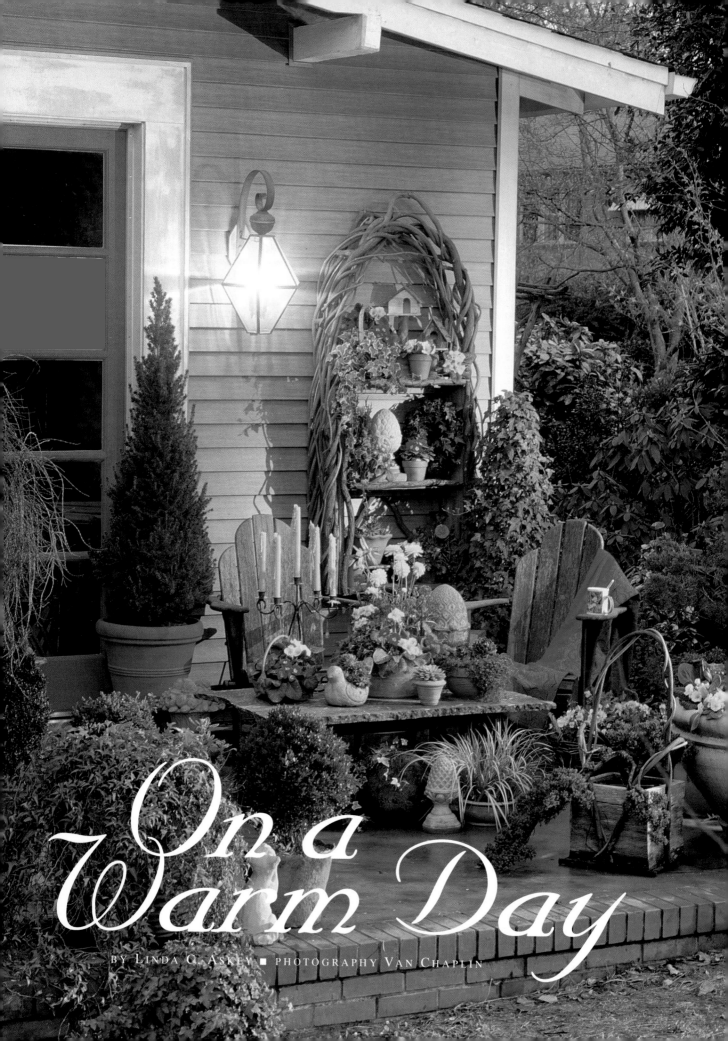

On a Warm Day

BY LINDA C. ASKEY ▪ PHOTOGRAPHY VAN CHAPLIN

Winter is welcome in the South. When the sky turns deep blue and the sunlight glints from the broad leaves of evergreens, a sheltered nook can trap the sun's warmth and give us respite from the usual four walls. That's when a little terrace, deck, or patio is at its best.

"I use my screened porch during the summer, but the only time I really use my terrace is in the winter," says Karin Purvis of Greenville, South Carolina. The cozy lap robe across a chair, the carefully tended colorful flowers, and the partially melted candles stand as testament to any hearth-hugging nonbelievers.

Keeping the terrace plantings attractive is the key. "When the leaves fall, many of us go in the house and shut the door," Karin says. "If you let your space outside get unattractive in winter, you don't want to go out there, even on a nice day. If you keep it inviting and interesting, you really can't wait."

Karin uses a variety of plants to keep her terrace looking good through the lean season. Follow her guidelines to find renewed pleasure on a warm winter day.

Evergreens are the backbone of a garden, but keeping them in containers in the winter is a novel idea for many.

> "I love that warm January day when you get the urge to be outside. I take a cup of coffee, my lunch, or a magazine. I enjoy being there because it's nice looking."
>
> —*Karin Purvis*

Karin plants hardy conifers, miniature English ivy topiaries, boxwoods, thyme, and hardy succulents in pots.

Furnishings elevate a piece of paving to an outdoor room. Ornaments can be whimsical as well as practical. Birdhouses are cheerful reminders of a warmer season, and candles add charm.

Flowers give a winter garden the spark of life that seems to be missing this time of year. Karin uses primulas and ranunculus, but violas and pansies will also endure. When the weather gets severe, she brings in the potted flowers and throws a sheet over planters that are too big to move.

Color can be found in more than just flowers. Try hardy vegetables such as radicchio, red mustard, lettuces, or ornamental kale and cabbage. Gardeners in the coldest areas of the South can select hardy shrubs with colorful bark, such as coral bark maple (*Acer palmatum* Sangokaku) or the red- or yellow-stemmed red-osier dogwood (*Cornus sericea*).

Fragrance adds an often overlooked dimension to any garden, but in winter it is particularly welcome. Karin grows winter daphne (*Daphne odora*) in a pot. The buds are colorful long before they open and release their delicious scent. Other choices include wintersweet (*Chimonanthus praecox*) and winter honeysuckle (*Lonicera fragrantissima*). And don't forget, yellow pansies and yellow primroses are remarkably sweet.

You'll probably want to grow other plants on your terrace during the warm months. Karin takes her evergreens and fragrant plants into the garden and sets them in borders. There they spend the summer until they again have a place of honor on her winter terrace. ◇

(Above, left) *These succulents look tender but are really cold tolerant.* **(Left)** *Japanese sweet flag* (Acorus gramineus Ogon) *is a surprisingly hardy garden perennial.*

Snowdrops (See page 43.)

February

Checklist for February

EDITORS' NOTEBOOK

Tick, tick, tick. If that last weird spell of mild winter weather woke your daffodils way too early, time could be running out. What should you do? Cover the bulbs? Cut them? As usual, I have all the answers. What to do depends on how far along your bulbs are. If they're just showing foliage, go back to sleep. A cold snap now won't stop them from blooming. But if your bulbs are blooming or the flower buds are showing color, listen to the weatherman and pray that for once he knows what he's talking about. If the expected low is 28 degrees or less, cut both budded and flowering stems now and enjoy them indoors. If it's only going down to 28.5 degrees, relax—my extensive research shows your daffodils will weather the cold just fine. And if they don't, you know whom to blame. That's right—your local weatherman.

Steve Bender

□ **Bananas**—To grow larger fruit, remove all but three to five hands (bunches) of bananas from a flowering stalk. For best results, do this after all the fruit is set, but before it gets more than a couple of inches long.

□ **Garden beds**—Plan and prepare beds for vegetables and annual flowers. Order seeds and buy plants for setting out in the weeks ahead. Careful planning can result in a long season of vegetable and flower production.

□ **Tour guide**—The Garden Conservancy has put together an Open Days Directory that can serve as your guide to some of the finest private gardens in our region. Call 1-888-842-2442 (toll free) to order.

□ **Valentine flowers**—To keep them fresh as long as possible, add water to the vase when the arrangement arrives, and check it daily. If they're in a box, snip an inch off each stem, remove leaves that will be below the water level of the vase, arrange, and enjoy.

□ **Volunteering**—One of the most fun ways to learn about gardening is to volunteer at a public garden. From working in the greenhouses to leading tours, there's sure to be a job you'll enjoy. When you call, ask for the volunteer coordinator. ▶

PLANT

◀ **Cool-weather annuals**—In Lower and Coastal South gardens, ornamental kale and cabbage, snapdragons, and sweet alyssum thrive during the cool months of late winter, so plant now.

□ **Blackberries**—Blackberries are a good choice for backyard gardens. Arapaho is a thornless type that is becoming popular, and Brazos and Rosborough are time-tested favorites. Select a sunny, well-drained area for best results.

□ **Blueberries**—Set out container-grown rabbit-eye types in the Middle and Lower South and highbush types in the Upper South. Blueberries prefer full sun but otherwise like the same conditions as azaleas: well-drained, slightly acid, organic soil.

□ **Flowers**—In the Middle and Lower South, set out transplants of pansies, violas, calendulas, forget-me-nots, snapdragons, poppies, sweet alyssum, sweet William, annual pinks, and bachelor's-buttons. In the Upper South, sow seeds of bachelor's-buttons, larkspur, sweet peas, and poppies when the soil can be worked.

□ **Grapes**—Muscadines are successful in most of the South. In addition to producing grapes, these vines are attractive, insect and disease resistant, and useful to cover arbors for summer shade and enclosure. Plant now for best results. ▶

◀ **Pineapple lily**—Plant these bulbs now for handsome foliage and intriguing blossoms. Bury the bulbs shallowly, just barely covering them with soil. They like partial shade and moisture. Be sure to water during drought. They'll bloom in four to five months.

☐ **Vegetables**—In the Middle and Lower South sow seeds of beets, carrots, radishes, turnips, spinach, mustard, and English and edible-podded peas this month. Set out transplants of cabbage, cauliflower, lettuce, onions, and potatoes, but wait until next month in the Upper South. In the Coastal South set out the first crop of tomatoes and peppers; be prepared to protect them from a late cold snap, however.

PRUNE

☐ **Bougainvillea**—At its peak of color right now in Coastal South gardens, bougainvillea will continue to flower through summer. To control its rapid growth, prune as needed. Because this shrub is so vigorous, don't be shy about cutting it back; new growth from pruning will form more blossoms by next winter. ▶

☐ **Flowering shrubs**—Overgrown, diseased, or damaged shrubs should be pruned just before new growth begins. However, if the plant blooms early, you will be cheating yourself of the flowers. Postpone pruning a few weeks and put your trimmings in a vase indoors.

☐ **Roses**—Everblooming roses, such as hybrid teas, floribundas, grandifloras, teas, polyanthas, and Chinas, should be pruned in the Lower and Coastal South early in February and by the end of the month in other parts of the state. Begin by removing any dead or weak canes. Leave three to five healthy canes, and cut them back to about 18 to 24 inches. Wait until after spring flowering has finished to prune climbers and once-blooming types.

☐ **Snapdragons**—Encourage snapdragons to grow more spikes from the beginning by pinching off the tops of young transplants when you first set them out. Snip the flower stalk off at its base, just before the topmost set of leaves.

CONTROL

☐ **Lawns**—Apply pre-emergence herbicides if your lawn has a history of crabgrass and other summer weeds. Treat the lawn before seeds germinate. Watch the forsythias in your neighborhood. Be sure to apply before they bloom.

FERTILIZE

☐ **Landscape plantings**—Feed ground covers, trees, and shrubs as they begin spring growth. Use a controlled-release fertilizer such as 12-6-6 according to label directions.

☐ **Palms**—To keep palms a healthy green, feed them with a palm food that contains iron, manganese, and magnesium. These nutrients are often lacking in sandy and alkaline soils, and a deficiency will make certain leaves turn yellow.

TOMATO
MAN

*Paul Newell really likes
tomatoes. And he grows them
like nobody's business.*

P aul Newell knows tomatoes like Bill Gates knows computers. Come to think of it, Paul knows tomatoes a whole lot better.

Since 1946, he's been growing them in his small backyard garden in Kosciusko, Mississippi. And he's become very, very good at it. Some of his plants top 20 feet tall. He picks the first tomatoes by about mid-May. His three-dozen plants bear more than 700 pounds of fruit a year. Obviously, Paul really likes tomatoes.

If you like them, too, and want to harvest more than you can stuff in a futon, read on. Paul is about to reveal his secrets.

SECRET TOMATO FORMULA FINALLY EXPOSED!
■ **Choose the right ones.** "The same kind of tomato won't grow good for everybody," says Paul. So choose selections that do well in your area. He grows Burpee's Early

Pick for an early harvest; then plants Crimson Fancy and SuperTasty for his main-season crop.

■ **For really early tomatoes, start really early.** Paul sows seeds for his earliest fruiting tomatoes in a small greenhouse during the first week of January. (The last frost usually occurs around April 20.) By February 22, he sows his main crop and transplants the early seedlings to his cold frame. The cold frame runs north-south; sheets of black plastic along its back gather solar warmth. A removable top and front let Paul adjust the temperature inside. On cold winter days, an electric heating coil warms the soil. Paul turns it on two to three weeks before planting. In

Paul's been keeping records of sowing and planting dates, as well as daily high and low temperatures, for more than 30 years.

mid-March, he pots up his main-season plants. He places them in the cold frame behind the earlier plants, until the weather's warm enough for the later transplants to go into the beds.

■ **Good soil is key.** Paul's original soil was hard clay. Now it's as soft as cake mix. Paul made it this way by tilling in about a *half-ton* of compost a year. His compost comes from a 20- x 4- x 4-foot bin that he fills with leaves. Each fall he gathers the leaves from the neighborhood and runs them through a shredder. Sprinkling a handful of nitrogen fertilizer atop each layer of leaves speeds decomposition.

■ **Plant 'em right.** Paul advises setting the plants into the ground so

BY STEVE BENDER ■ PHOTOGRAPHY VAN CHAPLIN

Key to early tomatoes is a cold frame to protect plants from frost. Black plastic gathers solar warmth, while the removable front and top allow Paul to adjust the temperature inside.

After digging a furrow for each row, Paul uses a tiller to loosen the soil and work in cottonseed meal and organic matter.

Pinching off suckers at the base directs the plant's energy into making fruit, producing an earlier crop.

After watering the container plants, he waters the bottom of the planting hole. After all, that's where the roots will be.

An inch or two of compost nourishes each new plant. It also helps warm the soil in spring, notes Paul.

that only the top set of leaves are showing. The plants will root along their buried stems, making them vigorous and drought tolerant. Some folks prefer digging a deep hole; others like laying the plant sideways in a shallow trench. Paul says deep holes work better in dry years, shallow trenches in wet years.

■ **Feed the hungry.** Growing tomatoes need lots of food. Before planting his main crop, Paul digs a foot-deep furrow for each row, sprinkles a good amount of cottonseed meal down the middle, and tills it in. He spreads an inch or two of compost around each tomato at planting. During the growing season, he sprinkles about a half-pound of 5-20-20 fertilizer beside each 35-foot row. He regularly sprays Harvest Alive! 2-1-1 on the leaves. And once a month, he waters each plant with a gallon of Miracle-Gro solution, to which he's added a tablespoon of Epsom salts.

■ **Water regularly.** Fruiting crops such as tomatoes won't bear well if their growth is checked. They need steady moisture. Paul supplies it by running soaker hoses down the center of each row.

■ **Control pests.** If grubs or bad nematodes plague your soil, add beneficial nematodes, which destroy these pests. Spray plants with Neem to repel chewing insects. Rake off and destroy pest-laden mulch after each growing season. And don't leave rotting fruit on the vine—it attracts pests.

EVEN THE TOMATO MAN HAS HIS LIMITS

You might wonder what someone does with 700 pounds of tomatoes each year. Paul and Yverlette, his wife of 59 years, give a lot away. They also eat a lot of tomato sandwiches. "Once, when our kitchen was being remodeled, we went three weeks without a stove," he recalls. "We ate nothing but tomato sandwiches." How did they fare? "We lost 15 pounds apiece." ◇

(For sources see pages 250–251.)

PHOTOGRAPH: SYLVIA MARTIN; (INSET) VAN CHAPLIN

Tired of plain, white potatoes? These three types grew well for us—All Blue (blue), Yukon Gold (yellow), and Bison (white flesh, red skin).

(Inset) *Mound soil around the plants periodically. This provides cool soil for the growing tubers.*

Really New Potatoes

"One potato, two potato, *blue potato,* four . . . "

Say what? Blue potatoes? That's right. Potatoes don't have to be white anymore. Now you can grow all sorts of gourmet types. Some are blue inside, some are yellow, some are red, and some are speckled. So if you're adventurous, need exercise, and have an insatiable hunger for blue food, here's how.

First, you need seed potatoes. One of the best sources is Ronniger's Seed Potatoes (P.O. Box 1838, Orting, WA 98360). While you're waiting for the tubers to arrive, prepare your soil. Potatoes need loose, fertile, well-drained soil that contains plenty of organic matter. It must be slightly acid (pH 6 to 6.8) because alkaline soil causes a disfiguring disease called scab. Use a tiller or garden fork to turn over the soil to a depth of at least 15 inches. Work in lots of sphagnum peat moss, compost, chopped leaves, and rotted cow manure. If your soil is alkaline (a soil test will tell you), add garden sulfur to acidify it.

Potatoes like cool weather. Thus, the farther south you live, the earlier you need to plant. Plant three to four weeks before your last expected frost, when the temperature of the soil has risen to at least 55 degrees.

First, dig a shallow trench that's about 10 inches deep and 2 feet wide. Space the trenches 2 feet apart. Set seed potatoes a foot apart. To get more plants, you can cut potatoes into wedges. Make sure each wedge has an eye. Also, let it sit out in the sun for a day before planting, so the cut surfaces can heal over. Plants grown from wedges produce just as many potatoes as those grown from whole potatoes.

Given good soil, potatoes need little fertilizer. Cottonseed meal sprinkled in the bottom of each trench at planting suffices. Use a rake to cover the seed potatoes with 4 inches of soil. When the new plants stand 8 inches tall, mound soil around them, so that only the top 4 inches show. When another 8 inches of stem are exposed, do this again. This produces a mound of cool soil where tubers form.

As soon as the weather gets really hot, the plants wither and die. Don't panic. Ignore them for two weeks—the tubers will "cure" in the ground. Then dig them up.

Some selections take hot Southern weather better than others. My top performers were All Blue (blue flesh and skin), Bison (white flesh, red skin), Caribe (white flesh, blue skin), Yukon Gold (yellow flesh and skin), and Candy Stripe (white flesh, red-striped skin). But before you run and order, keep in mind that growing potatoes is labor-intensive, while buying regular, store-bought ones is easy *and* cheap. The only reason to grow the gourmet types is if, like me, you're just dying for blue food.

Steve Bender

A LITTLE BIT OF *Style*

Tucked behind a bungalow, this tiny garden takes on classic proportions.

BY JO KELLUM
PHOTOGRAPHY
JEAN ALLSOPP

It's one of those small gardens done with such taste that even Winston, the elderly cat who patrols it, complements the understated color scheme. From the well-appointed back porch and boxwood-lined brick paths to the pergola framing a borrowed view of a neighboring field, style stakes its claim in every square inch.

It was the view that started it all. Interior decorator Randy Roper renovated his home in Huntsville, Alabama's historic district. That done, he turned his attention to the small lot. An old outbuilding took up much of the room in the 39-foot-deep backyard.

(Inset) *A peaked pergola straddles the spot where an outbuilding once stood. Viewed from the porch, the pergola frames the backdrop of a neighboring field.*

(Above, right) *The cat's meow: Morning sun makes the porch a favorite spot to overlook the garden.*

Randy demolished the building and unveiled a priceless gardening prize: a view that stretched across his garden to a tree-shaded field behind his property.

This revelation changed the garden much the way peeling off a layer of old wallpaper and discovering a hand-painted mural would change a room. Randy called garden designer Bill Nance, whose first step was to create a pergola to frame the vista.

The wooden structure borrows its lines and column details from the back of the house. The terrace beneath the pergola gives Randy plenty of room for entertaining. Deep shade dictated an all-green gardening theme, which suits Randy fine. Boxwood, ivy topiaries, and hosta lend the garden a subdued formality. "In a small space like this one, there's not room for competing colors," says Randy. "I put two round tables under the pergola when I entertain and that's where I want my color, in tablecloths and flower arrangements."

If guests are lucky, Winston will pose, a purring study in black and white. He may be the ultimate garden accessory. ◇

COLOR SCHEMING

Contrasting colors can make a small garden seem even smaller. Randy chose his paint colors carefully to make his house part of the garden.

Siding: Benjamin Moore #1538

Trim, columns, and pergola: Benjamin Moore #HC84

Shutters: Market Square Tavern by Martin-Senour

Displaying Daffodils

Use one of your loveliest porcelain bowls or jars to hold a creative combination of bulbs and daffodils. Fill the bowl with saturated florist foam, and add a layer of papery brown bulbs. Finish the arrangement by inserting freshly picked daffodil stems into the foam. The effect is of early spring flowers that have just emerged.

Bulbs need their leaves to produce nutrients for growth, and cutting daffodils can damage the foliage. Instead, just pick the flowers with your fingers. The upper portion of the stem is hollow and won't hold moisture, so reach down to the white part of the stem, and snap it off. Be sure to leave foliage intact.

Arranged flowers should stay cool, away from a dry heat source, and out of direct sunlight. Cooler night temperatures also help keep them fresh. Place the arrangement near a window at night; the flowers can tolerate temperatures to about 28 degrees.

Julia H. Thomason

PHOTOGRAPHS: JEAN ALLSOPP / STYLING: MICHAEL HABRAT

TOOLS & MATERIALS

florist foam
decorative container
knife
daffodil bulbs
pencil
daffodil blossoms

Step 1: SATURATE a block of florist foam. Insert the foam in a decorative container, cutting it to fit about ½ inch below the rim. Add water.

Step 2: ARRANGE bulbs over the surface of the foam. Pierce the foam with a pencil, and insert the flower stems.

Arrange daffodils in a decorative bowl, and place them in front of a mirror to double their effect. Small containers require fewer flowers, and you can feature them on a tabletop, in a bookshelf, or on a mantel. Include other kinds of blooms when they're available.

A Rosey Valentine Centerpiece

Valentine's Day is a dress-up holiday. We wear our frilly best, add romance to our tables, and indulge in fancy menus. Spiff up an ivy topiary for a centerpiece that's easy and elegant. Afterwards, you'll have a houseplant to enjoy.

ROSE PETAL CONTAINER

Purchase roses to dry, or dry garden roses during summer months. Dried rose petals also may be used as an ingredient in potpourri. Air-dry roses by hanging from the stem upside-down in a dry place, or try this faster method.

1 Cut the stems of roses 1 inch below blooms. Place through slots on top shelf of food dehydrator. If you're drying large blooms, use only the top shelf. Lower shelves can be used when the flowers are small. Carefully stack shelves without crushing any blooms. Place the top on the dehydrator, and turn on. Roses will be completely dried in about 24 hours. Flowers may be left whole or pulled apart into rose petals. Store in a zip-top plastic bag.

2 Glue dried petals to the 5-inch clay pot, starting at the bottom and working up to the top. Overlap petals slightly. Once complete, place the vinyl saucer inside the pot.

TOPIARY

1 To give the finished topiary extra support, push a green garden stake into the pot along the "stem" and up into the ball at top. Gently tie the stake to the topiary with raffia or twine. Add birch branches around the stem for additional support and to fatten the appearance of the stem. Secure with raffia or twine.

2 Place the topiary in the covered pot, and secure with Spanish moss around edges. Fill water picks with water, and secure tops. Cut rose stems to appropriate length to fit in picks and stay in water. Push the water picks into the top of the topiary. The wire form and ivy will hold the roses and picks in place. Roses of different sizes and colors may be used. Spanish moss can be tucked between flowers to soften the appearance. Add a rose or two at the bottom of the topiary, and crisscross coordinating ribbon around the birch stems.

Roses will stay fresh in the water picks for several days. To keep the ivy topiary healthy, remove the flowers after several days. However, the rose-covered pot can be used as an accent year-round. *Ellen Riley*

An ivy topiary is transformed into a festive centerpiece with a few simple supplies.

TOOLS & MATERIALS

roses for drying

food dehydrator

zip-top plastic bag

hot-glue gun

1 (5-inch) clay pot

1 (4-inch) vinyl saucer

1 (12-inch-tall) ivy topiary in 4½-inch pot

1 (12-inch) green garden stake

raffia or green garden twine

birch branches

Spanish moss

water picks

7 or more large roses, or smaller spray roses

ribbon

This handsome planter was made by covering a plastic foam cooler with a mixture of Portland cement, peat moss, sand, and water.

Catherine Webster

Make a Trough Garden

If you've got a free afternoon and don't mind making a mess, here's a project for you. Catherine Webster of Savannah shared her instructions for making a trough garden after I admired one on her patio.

The planter's rough texture resembles English stone troughs, once used for feeding livestock and now in great demand for container gardening. Making your own is considerably less expensive and more fun.

Note: The size of your plastic foam cooler determines the finished size of your planter. It also determines the amount of cement mixture you will need (see Step 6).

Step 1: Lay the plywood down to protect your deck or patio. You can work directly on the wood.

Step 2: Cut the sides of the cooler down, leaving it approximately 4- to 6-inches deep.

Step 3: Wrap the cooler with chicken wire, folding the edges under so a couple of inches are inside the cooler. Poke the sharp ends into the plastic foam to secure.

Step 4: Invert cooler and poke holes in bottom with screwdriver. Press dowels through holes so they are half in and half out. (You will remove the dowels in Step 9, forming drainage holes for your planter.)

Step 5: Form a thick mound of wet sand slightly larger than the mouth of your cooler. Invert cooler and press into sand to leave imprint. Dig a moat in sand slightly wider than the imprint. Cover sand with plastic sheeting.

Step 6: Combine 1 part Portland cement; 2 parts sand; and 2 parts peat moss, with large chunks removed. Add enough water to make mixture thick and wet, like cottage cheese. Mixture will look dark.

Step 7: Fill plastic-covered moat with cement mixture. Invert cooler and press it into cement mixture.

Step 8: Press remaining mixture onto sides and bottom of cooler until no chicken wire is visible. Cover entire project with plastic.

Step 9: Remove plastic after a day or so, and check your trough for hardening. When cement mixture is firm but can be dented with your fingernail, your planter is prime for texturizing. Remove dowels.

Step 10: Use a wire brush and screwdriver to roughen the surface of your trough, giving it an aged appearance. Round off sharp corners.

Step 11: Let planter continue to harden without plastic sheeting. Leave plastic foam inside planter, and fill with potting soil as soon as cement mixture is fully hardened. Add your favorite plants. *Jo Kellum*

TOOLS & MATERIALS

- small sheet of inexpensive plywood
- plastic foam cooler
- sharp knife
- chicken wire and wire cutters
- screwdriver
- 1-inch wooden dowel, cut in 4 equal lengths
- sand or vermiculite
- plastic sheeting
- Portland cement (not a sand mixture)
- peat moss
- water
- wire brush

Perennial Primer

No garden is more dependable than one that's liberally stocked with perennials. These plants are available in crayon colors and boast season-long flowering times—from spring's first warm breath to fall's last, lingering frost. And best of all, a well-tended perennial bed wraps the earth in a coverlet of hue and blossom that grows fuller and more beautiful through the years.

Creating your own perennial paradise is no mystery. It doesn't require a large growing area or a degree in horticulture. By carefully selecting your plants you can easily stage a show in your garden that's guaranteed to steal the neighborhood spotlight. Our tips will help you get started and keep your garden looking its best, year after year.

Perennials prefer soil that's rich and well drained. You can improve on Mother Nature's soil recipe in your garden by adding organic material in the form of composted manure, leaf compost, or peat moss. If your soil isn't sandy to start with, adding sand can enhance drainage. Organic fertilizers such as cottonseed meal or bonemeal will create a nutrient-packed soil perfect for hungry roots.

Soon after the first crocuses poke through the ground to brighten winter's drab palette, spend some time cleaning your perennial patch. Remove last year's stalks, leaves, or any other material that has collected around overwintering plants. Take care to cut perennial stalks—instead of pulling them—so you don't damage young, growing roots or emerging shoots. Late winter is a great time to tackle weeds. Remove seedlings as they emerge, before they have a chance to become established in the garden.

Although fall is the best time to plant perennials, you can add them to your garden in early spring too. Spring-planted ones may not bloom much the first year, but will take a starring role in the garden in their second growing season. For a quicker show of flowers, plant gallon-size perennials or large divisions from mature plants.

Divide late-summer and fall-blooming perennials, such as black-eyed Susan, Autumn Joy sedum, or aster before the growing season starts. Divide crowded clumps of spring bloomers when flowering is finished. Feed established plants every spring by working well-aged compost or manure into the soil around plants with a weeding claw.

Once flowers begin to unfold, extend the blooming season by faithfully removing spent blossoms. Perennials such as coralbells, veronica, and coreopsis will continue to flower well into the growing season as long as they aren't allowed to set seed.

Give your perennial garden pizzazz by borrowing design tips from the professionals. Plant in groups of three or five for visual impact, stair-step color (tall plants in back, low-growing ones in front), and curve the edges of your planting beds.

Julie A. Martens

PHOTOGRAPH: TINA CORNETT; (INSET): VAN CHAPLIN

(Above) *Pair the towering spires of baptisia with bearded iris and peonies to transform your perennial bed into a work of art.* **(Inset)** *Late-summer gardens come to life with vibrant black-eyed Susans. The lime-green flowers of Autumn Joy sedum weather to a burgundy-bronze in fall.*

If the phrase winter garden seems like a contradiction, consider the border this Charlotte couple has created.

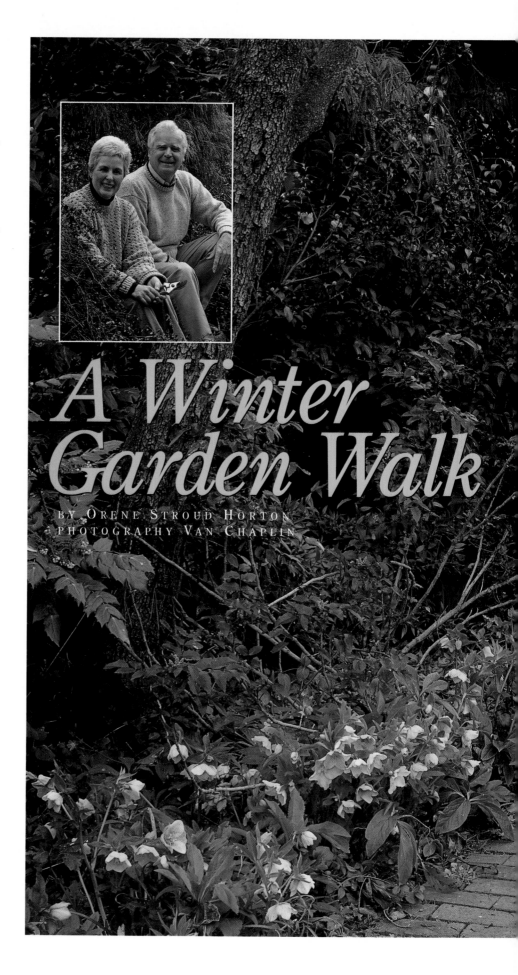

A Winter Garden Walk

BY ORENE STROUD HORTON
PHOTOGRAPHY VAN CHAPLIN

This time of year most gardeners are toasting their toes by the fire and dreaming of spring. But Genie and Jim White are already outside. Designed with winter in mind, their garden pathway meanders through plantings featuring berries and buds. Sweet fragrance drifts on cold currents of air, inviting these dedicated gardeners to step outside daily and greet each new flower that opens.

Even on the coldest days, when frost-flecked winds keep them inside, they enjoy their garden. "We look at it from the windows of our den, the room where we stay so much of the wintertime with the fireplace and all," says Genie. "The border gets pretty light from the sun, so everything is highlighted."

About a dozen years ago garden designer Phyllis Herring suggested they plant a winter border. "She

Mahonia, Lenten roses, Jet Trail quince, and Japanese black pine make an inviting pathway.

Daffodils and pansies (See page 64.)

March

Checklist
for
March

EDITORS' NOTEBOOK

Don't eat this pizza. And don't plant it either. What the heck am I babbling about? Well, folks in the South really love azaleas—so much so that they plant one of every color all together. I call it the "pizza with everything" look. They start with a base of hot pink azaleas, ladle on a layer of orange and red, sprinkle some purple ones around, then top it off with white. "Wish someone made a yellow or green azalea," they mutter. "Then I could call my garden 'The Works.' " Friends, if you want a garden that really works, stick to two or three harmonious colors and masses of single colors. Trust me, the result will be even tastier. And you won't have to pick out the anchovies.

Steve Bender

☐ **Azaleas**—Choose your plants while they're in bloom so that colors can be effectively combined. Partially shaded locations are best. Well-drained soils enriched with organic material such as peat, composted pine bark, or compost help retain moisture during the dry months of summer. Indica azaleas, such as Formosa, George Lindley Taber, and Mrs. G. G. Gerbing, may grow 6 to 8 feet tall with a similar spread, while Kurume and Glenn Dale hybrids usually range from 2 to 5 feet at maturity.

☐ **Birdhouses**—Get birdhouses and feeders out now so early arrivals will choose your garden for their nesting sites. Even if migrating birds don't stay around, you'll have an interesting parade of species to observe through the spring months.

☐ **Frost date**—If you don't know the date frost typically leaves your area, ask your county Extension office, garden center, or local botanical garden. Knowing this date will help you judge when it is time to set out tender plants, fertilize, and prune.

☐ **Annuals**—Begonias, impatiens, geraniums, petunias, marigolds, zinnias, cleome, and other warm-weather annuals may be set out now in the Lower and Coastal South. They prefer well-prepared beds where several inches of peat, composted pine bark, or compost have been spaded or tilled. Add 2 or 3 pounds of organic or commercial fertilizer per 100 square feet of bed area.

☐ **Blueberries**—Plant a row of blueberries, such as Southland, Delite, Woodward, or Sharpblue, as a handsome fruiting hedge. It will reward you with fruit in summer and bright red foliage in fall. The first year, remove any berries that form; this lets the plant put energy into growing larger.

☐ **Butterflies**—Four plants sure to encourage butterflies to visit your garden are lantana, zinnia, pentas, and butterfly bush. Be sure to plant these in full sun. If placed in the same bed, the mass of color will attract more winged beauties.

☐ **Flowering shrubs**—Mock orange, bridal wreath, flowering quince, forsythia, and other spring-flowering shrubs are available in easy-to-transplant containers and are minimum-care sources of spring color. Sunny or partially shaded locations are ideal for placing most flowering shrubs in groups or masses. ▶

☐ **Hostas**—Divide and replant mature clumps as new growth begins. If you do it now, they will fill out and you won't be able to tell they were divided.

☐ **Roses**—The selection of rose plants at your garden center is at its best now. Look for old favorites, as well as new ones, offering fragrance and disease tolerance. Consider how you can use roses as climbers and shrubs. Soak bare-root roses in a bucket of water overnight before planting them in the garden.

◀ **Vegetables**—Warm-weather vegetables such as tomatoes, peppers, eggplants, squash, and cucumbers may be set out as soon as the last average frost date for your area has passed. Freezes can and do still occur, but early plantings are usually worth some risk. You can set out transplants of cold crops such as

broccoli, cabbage, and cauliflower up to four weeks before the last spring frost in your area. Sow seeds of carrots, radishes, spinach, turnips, and leaf lettuce at the same time.

☐ **Warm-weather plants**—Hibiscus, bougainvillea, caladiums, coleus, and other warm-weather plants can be set out now in the Lower and Coastal South for landscape color that lasts all season.

◄ **Zinnias**—Sow seeds of zinnias as soon as the danger of frost has passed. Tall types for cutting are usually best grown by direct seeding. If you sow a few seeds every month through July, you can have fresh flowers through October.

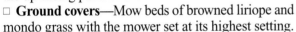

PRUNE

☐ **Fruit trees**—Apple and peach trees need careful pruning to benefit the trees and enhance their fruit production. Remove all suckers from the base of the tree, as well as dead, crossed, or vigorous upright shoots called water sprouts. Apples and pears should have a central leader that results in a cone-shaped tree, while peaches should have open center branches like the up-facing palm of a hand. ►

☐ **Ground covers**—Mow beds of browned liriope and mondo grass with the mower set at its highest setting. A nylon-string trimmer is also effective. Be sure to get the job done before new foliage has begun to grow, or you'll have brown tips on each new leaf for the coming year.

CONTROL

☐ **Weedy seedlings**—Don't allow tree seedlings or other weeds that sprout in ground cover beds to take over. Pull them now before they become more firmly rooted. Tree seedlings in beds of ground cover such as mondo grass or Asian star jasmine are easy to kill by mowing.

FERTILIZE

◄ **Cool-weather annuals**—Fertilize violas, pansies, and other overwintering annuals as the weather warms and growth begins. Use a slow-release fertilizer such as 9-6-6 for the remainder of spring, or give them a quick start with liquid 20-20-20.

☐ **Orchids**—Give orchids the bright, filtered light they need by hanging them from the lower branches of oak trees or placing them under another low-branched tree or in a south-facing window. Feed with a diluted liquid orchid fertilizer through spring to encourage growth, especially on plants that have spent the winter indoors.

☐ **Soil test**—The best way to determine fertilizer needs for lawns and gardens is to test your soil. Contact your county Extension agent or local nursery for information and a soil test kit. Results include specific recommendations tailored to your needs. This can save you money and help protect the environment.

TIP OF THE MONTH

I discovered an easy way to keep cats from digging in our herb bed. I bought some lightweight, black netting and placed pieces of the material on the ground around our plants. The fabric allows penetration by both water and plants, but cats can't dig through it.

JANE HALFORD
MOUNT PLEASANT, SOUTH CAROLINA

parade of
lettuce

Crisp and fresh, lettuce is the grand marshal of the spring garden.

Marchfrom early spring straight into summertime with a rollicking cavalcade of lettuce that will delight both the palate and the eye. Start up the parade now with cold-tolerant selections. Make the first turn into spring with cool-weather types, and then bring up the rear in early summer with those that tolerate some heat. Equally at home in the vegetable garden or flower border, lettuce presents garden-fresh flavors and jewellike colors that money just can't buy.

HOW TO GROW
Choose a location that receives direct sunlight for a minimum of four to six hours. Lettuce requires rich, well-drained soil. Amend clay soils with compost or finely ground bark. Lucinda Mays, of Callaway

BY ELLEN RILEY
PHOTOGRAPHY JEAN
ALLSOPP, VAN CHAPLIN

Gardens in Pine Mountain, Georgia, plants radish seeds with lettuce. "Radishes punch through the heavy clay soil and make growth easier for the maturing lettuce. Radishes mature in 21 days and are harvested about halfway through lettuce's growth cycle."

The most economical way to obtain the greatest variety of selections is to grow lettuce from seeds. Purchased transplants are faster, but your choices may be fewer.

Lettuce seeds germinate best in cool soil. In Jefferson, Georgia, Virgil Adams begins planting seeds in his garden in late January. He sows more every two to three weeks. "Lettuce seeds are very inexpensive. If I don't have a successful crop on the first planting, the next will probably fare better. I've heard that if you plant in late winter and *don't* lose any plants to a freeze, you've started too late."

Holly Shimizu of Richmond begins planting seed in mid-March. In Houston, Camille Waters *begins* seeding lettuce in October, and plants her last crop around mid-February. In Pine Mountain, Georgia, Lucinda says for a sure crop, begin seeding two to four weeks before the last frost date.

Lettuce seeds require light to germinate. Sprinkle seeds on top of the soil, and lightly cover or scratch them into the bed just below the surface of the soil. Lettuce must be kept moist throughout its growing season.

As seedlings mature, they need to be thinned. When they are 2 or 3 inches tall, gently pull out the largest plants. Camille regularly uses these for her first salad. "Even though the leaves are small, clean them well, and use in a salad—roots and all." Leave 6 to 8 inches between the remaining plants for sufficient room to mature. If pulling the seedlings is difficult, pinch them off instead.

Brightly colored snapdragons and poppies pair well with these cold-tolerant lettuces.

ROUGE D'HIVER

Cold-Weather Lettuce:

Rouge d'Hiver, red, romaine-type

Arctic King, green, semi-heading

Winter Marvel, green, semi-heading

TOM THUMB

Cool-Weather Lettuce:

Tom Thumb, green, semi-heading

Royal Oak Leaf, green, leaf lettuce

Lolla Rossa, red, leaf lettuce

TWO STAR

Heat-Tolerant Lettuce:

Two Star, green, leaf lettuce

Red Riding Hood, red, semi-heading

Black Seeded Simpson, green, leaf lettuce

Grow an entire salad in a pot, with selections of lettuce, edible nasturtiums, and herbs.

HARVESTTIME

Expect to begin harvesting leaf lettuce 45 days after planting, semi-heading selections in about 50 days. Harvest lettuce from the outside leaves first. The plant will continue to grow and produce more leaves. Or cut the entire plant 2 inches above its base. The new plants may not have the form of the original, but more harvestable leaves will be produced. Camille soaks harvested lettuce in an ice water bath for 5 minutes right after she picks it. She then drains the lettuce well and stores it in the refrigerator in plastic bags.

CONVENIENT CONTAINERS

Holly and Lucinda also grow lettuce in containers. Holly seeds lettuce directly into large pots on her deck. Other early-spring greens, such as arugula and cilantro, are added to the lettuce, along with a few nasturtiums or calendula seeds. "I can harvest fresh lettuce from the pots on my deck without ever putting my shoes on," Holly says.

Lucinda begins seeds indoors in peat pots in midwinter. She plants five to seven seeds per pot. As the seedlings grow, she transplants them into larger terracotta containers. "On warm days they all move outdoors for some sunshine. On nasty days, they're inside with me," she says. For whatever trouble this may seem to be, Lucinda has fresh lettuce right at her doorstep.

WINDING DOWN

With warmer days and nights, lettuce begins to bolt. It grows tall and becomes bitter. Then it will bloom and set seed. The parade is winding down, and it's time to pull the lettuce out of your garden or containers.

Begin the parade again in the early fall using the same planting tips. Start the procession with the heat-tolerant varieties, and bring up the rear with the cold-tolerant selections.

(For sources see pages 250–251.)

Gardening Answers

Solutions
to many common
**gardening
problems**

Gardens don't have to be in the front or back
Try a little **something special** on the side

BEFORE

AFTER

Above: A fence built inside the property line left room for planting dogwoods along the back side. Annuals and perennials give the area color.

The side yard may be the most overlooked spot on your property. But it doesn't have to be that way. Take a look at the garden Sherry Dahrling of Chattanooga grows in the sliver of soil bordering her driveway.

It wasn't always as inviting. When Sherry first started working on her side yard, it wasn't much more than a continuation of her neighbor's yard. The scene from her driveway, where family and friends formed their first impressions, was a grand view of the neighbor's swing set. But that didn't deter Sherry. She merely designed her own scalloped picket fence to grace the property line. Though the fence isn't tall enough to provide total privacy, it neatly defines the side yard. A gate leads to the neighbor's yard, keeping things friendly.

Sherry saw the sloping soil as an asset. Filling it with flowers, she turned the empty bank into a gallery of color. Lilies, iris, and annuals thrive there. Dogwoods add a leafy canopy above the fence. A rusty, old bicycle, propped beside the gate, adds a touch of whimsy. Sherry lined its basket with sphagnum moss and potting soil and turned it into a planter.

Now the first thing visitors see when they drive up is a charming garden. It's worth a second look. 🌿

Above: An old bicycle basket elevates flowers to new heights.

Left: Oriental lilies find a home in the side yard.

SIDE YARD SAVVY

■ Don't be afraid to close in the side yard. Fences, trees, and evergreen shrubs can help define a narrow space and establish privacy.

■ Use your privacy screen as a background for added interest up front. Pathways, flowers, ground covers, and shrubs will focus attention on your side of the property.

■ Pay attention to the angle from which the area is seen. You may view it most often from a driveway, from the backyard, or from a window within your house. Add a flowering tree, bench, or sculpture to the most visible spot so you can enjoy it.

Don't plant
grass where grass
won't grow

Grass will do a lot of things, but growing under trees isn't one of them. English ivy does a much better job.

Homeowners could save themselves a lot of trouble by remembering three little words—grass needs sun. It won't look good in shade, no matter what. So plant a shade-tolerant ground cover instead. There are plenty of choices that stay green all year and need little care.

English ivy *(Hedera helix)* is a favorite of garden designer Ron Deal of Classic City Gardens in Athens, Georgia. As you can see in the photo at left, he used it to carpet the ground beneath large oaks where the grass refused to grow. The ivy defines the planting bed and separates it from the lawn. Ron says that once ivy becomes established, it needs very little maintenance and weeding. "But if you let it get out of control, it's a nightmare," he warns. His advice—use a nylon-string trimmer now and then to keep the ivy from spreading.

According to landscape architect Naud Burnett, the number one ground cover in Dallas is Asian star jasmine *(Trachelospermum asiaticum)*. Why? "It's hardy, evergreen, has no insect or disease problems, fills in quickly, and grows in sun or shade," he says.

In the photo on page 57, Naud used Asian star jasmine to blanket the ground beneath a huge tree. Periodic trimming with a nylon-string trimmer keeps it in bounds. If you use this ground cover to border a lawn, you'll find its dark green color contrasts nicely with the lighter greens of St. Augustine, Zoysia, and centipede grass.

For gardeners in the Coastal and Tropical South, landscape architect Bob

Hartwig of Jacksonville, Florida, recommends wedelia *(Wedelia trilobata)*. This fast-spreading ground cover thrives in sun or light shade, blooms continuously in warm weather, and tolerates almost any well-drained soil. "It's very invasive," he warns, "but if you plant it in a wild or contained area, it can be very satisfactory."

The photo above demonstrates his point. Here a sweep of wedelia ties together a planting of live oak, pittosporum, and palmetto. Bob also likes using it on steep banks to control erosion.

Use a lawnmower or nylon-string trimmer to cut back these ground covers in late winter. This rejuvenates tired foliage. It also keeps the planting from growing too tall and mounding.

Give shade-tolerant ground covers a try. And save the grass for the sun. 🌿

(For sources see pages 250–251.)

Above, left: Wedelia blooms nearly continuously in the Coastal and Tropical South.

Above, right: Asian star jasmine fills in quickly and chokes out weeds.

MADE FOR THE SHADE

Name	Height	Growth Rate	Areas Adapted	Comments
Algerian ivy (*Hedera canariensis*)	8-10"	rapid	CS, TS	larger leaves than English ivy; more open in habit; will climb
Asian star jasmine (*Trachelospermum asiaticum*)	10-14"	rapid	LS, CS, TS	tough, easy-to-grow; will climb
common periwinkle (*Vinca minor*)	3-6"	moderate to rapid	US, MS, LS	attractive blue, purple, or white spring flowers
English ivy (*Hedera helix*)	6-10"	rapid once established	US, MS, LS, CS	will climb; susceptible to leaf spot if kept too wet
Japanese pachysandra (*Pachysandra terminalis*)	6-12"	slow	US, MS, LS	needs rich, moist, acid, well-drained soil
liriope (*Liriope sp.*)	12-24"	moderate	AS	tough, easy-to-grow; blue, purple, or white summer flowers
mondo grass (*Ophiopogon japonicus*)	3-10"	moderate	MS, LS, CS, TS	carefree; looks like dark green grass; fine texture
wedelia (*Wedelia trilobata*)	12-15"	rapid	CS, TS	Yellow, daisylike blooms appear continuously in warm weather.

AS=All South, CS=Coastal South, LS=Lower South, MS=Middle South, TS=Tropical South, US=Upper South

Mow that steep slope nevermore

If you think you pay too much for insurance now, just wait until your friendly agent watches you mow that steep slope out front. Your rates might shoot through the roof.

"But what am I supposed to do?" you ask. "I don't have the money to build terraces and retaining walls, and the neighbors will complain if I let the grass go." Answer—plant something other than grass that looks good, covers and holds the soil, and doesn't need to be mowed.

Plenty of ground covers, low shrubs, and perennials fill the bill—see "Plants You Can Bank On" on page 59 for some ideas. These plants may take a couple of years to cover completely; you will have to weed in the meantime. Eventually, though, upkeep on your slope will be minimal.

Before you replace the grass, however, measure the slope to estimate its steepness. A slope with a grade of 25% or less (1-foot rise for every 4 feet the slope goes back) is okay to mow. A 30% grade is borderline. A 33% grade

(1-foot rise for every 3 feet of slope) and higher is too steep. You stand a good chance of slipping, turning over your lawnmower, and losing some of your original equipment.

If you feel uncomfortable mowing and determine your slope is too steep to tackle safely, you'll need to get rid of the grass. You can do this by spraying it with Roundup or Finale according to label directions. Trouble is, bare slopes have a nasty habit of eroding during heavy rain. And whatever you plant won't hold the soil completely for a year or two.

Birmingham landscape architect Tommy Holcombe has a solution. "One way that's worked

for me is to put down a heavy layer of pine straw," he says. "Put it down thick [3 to 4 inches] because you only want to do it once. Then cover the slope with chicken wire and stake it down. This holds the pine straw in place. Next, use wire cutters to cut holes in the chicken wire where you need to plant. Then put plants in the ground. After about a month, the wire changes from being shiny to barely noticeable. And eventually, it rusts away." By that time, the plants have knitted together and completely covered your slope. If you have a slope that children might play on, use jute mesh instead of chicken wire.

DESIGN: BOB HARTWIG, JACKSONVILLE, FLORIDA

Above: Imagine mowing this slope around all the tree trunks. A lush ground cover of Asian star jasmine eliminates the work.

Left: Planted slopes don't have to be green and boring. Here yellow daylilies add bright color, while ornamental grasses contribute soft, billowing foliage.

Above: This solid planting of shore juniper (*Juniperus conferta*) solves the dangerous mowing problem nicely.

Pine straw is the mulch of choice on a slope, according to Tommy, because it doesn't wash away during a rain. Shredded bark isn't as good a choice. Pine bark chips shouldn't be used at all—they wash right off.

Watering plants on a slope can be difficult because much of the water simply runs off. Tommy has a suggestion for this too. If you have a sophisticated irrigation system, try watering the slope for approximately 10 minutes through several cycles, rather than watering continuously for an hour. This allows the water to soak in slowly. If you don't have an irrigation system, use soaker hoses or "leaky" hoses that water slowly and gently. 🌱

PLANTS YOU CAN BANK ON

Common name	Botanical name	Areas Adapted
Algerian ivy	(*Hedera canariensis*)	CS, TS
Asian star jasmine	(*Trachelospermum asiaticum*)	LS, CS, TS
cape honeysuckle	(*Tecomaria capensis*)	CS, TS
common periwinkle	(*Vinca minor*)	US, MS, LS, CS
daylily	(*Hemerocallis* sp.)	AS
English ivy	(*Hedera helix*)	US, MS, LS, CS
holly fern	(*Cyrtomium falcatum*)	LS, CS, TS
juniper	(*Juniperus* sp.)	US, MS, LS, CS
liriope	(*Liriope* sp.)	AS
ornamental grasses		AS
spreading English yew	(*Taxus baccata* Repandens)	US, MS
wedelia	(*Wedelia trilobata*)	CS, TS
weeping forsythia	(*Forsythia suspensa* Sieboldii)	US, MS, LS
willowleaf cotoneaster	(*Cotoneaster salicifolius*)	US, MS, LS
wintercreeper euonymus	(*Euonymus fortunei*)	US, MS, LS
winter jasmine	(*Jasminum nudiflorum*)	US, MS, LS, CS

AS-All South, CS-Coastal South, LS-Lower South, MS-Middle South, US-Upper South

A weed-free lawn begins with the basics

A lawn appears healthy when it has no weeds. But to tell the truth, it's the other way around. A lawn has no weeds *because* it's healthy.

"Vigorous turf is the best weed control," says Dr. Richard White of Texas A&M University. "Proper fertilization, mowing, and irrigation will improve the density of the desirable grasses."

Sometimes weeds are just a symptom of a bigger problem. If the lawn has been scalped, the turf is weak and the soil is exposed. Treating it with an herbicide will kill the weeds on hand, but unless the cutting height of the lawnmower is raised, the grass will not grow back to compete with future weeds.

MAINTENANCE BASICS

Fertilizer: Applying too little will leave your lawn starved and stunted, and weeds will invade. Use too much fertilizer, and your lawn will be succulent and more susceptible to disease. For best results, follow label directions for your type of grass.

Mowing: Cutting height varies with the type of grass you are growing. If you cut a St. Augustine lawn to 1 inch, you will have more weed problems than if you mowed it 2½ inches tall. The proper cutting height ranges are as follows.

common Bermuda	1 to 1½ inches
centipede	1½ to 2 inches
Kentucky bluegrass	2 to 2½ inches
St. Augustine	2½ to 3 inches
tall fescue	2 to 3 inches
Zoysia	1 to 2 inches

Watering: The ideal lawn is thick and deep-rooted so that it can tolerate moderate droughts without your intervention. However, when your lawn needs help, water until the soil is moist 4 to 6 inches deep. If you don't know how deep the water has penetrated, go get a shovel. Check it hourly and see. If the water runs off before then, turn it off for a while and then water again. If your lawn is deeply rooted, it will be able to survive while young weeds dry out and die.

CHEMICAL WARFARE

Good lawn maintenance will eliminate many problems without relying on a chemical arsenal. Herbicides should be used only as needed. When you know the weeds and their seeds are present in abundance, a well-timed application of the right product will give your lawn the head start it needs. It is important to know the kind of lawn you have, and to know the weeds. If you have doubts about either one, take a sample to the garden center and ask for help. When you buy an herbicide, you have a choice.

Pre-emergence weed control must be applied before the weed seeds germinate. Use this type of product only if weeds have been a problem in the past. Apply it in early spring, just before forsythia blooms, to catch crabgrass and other summer weeds. In late summer as the night temperature begins to cool, apply herbicide to catch the annual bluegrass, dandelion, and other winter weeds.

Post-emergence weed control kills weeds after they are already visible. Although weed-and-feed products save you time, Dr. White recommends using a spray herbicide for best results. If you use a granular product, opt for the brand with the smallest particles.

Always read the label carefully to be sure the product is recommended for your type of lawn. 🌿

Reroute your
downspout

Underneath this colorful flowerbed, a pipe carries water from the downspout to the side of the house.

This neat little flowerbed has all the downspout water piped underneath it. Its flowers look much more attractive than the plastic pipe that had been laid in front of this home.

It's important to move water around your house, preventing it from seeping into your basement or foundation. Burying your pipes underground is an attractive solution. We'll show you how.

■ First remove the black plastic pipe leading from the downspout, and measure how many feet of new pipe are needed. Check to see if you'll need any 90-degree elbow joints for turning corners and attaching to the downspouts.

■ Buy slick PVC pipe instead of a perforated black pipe. The black pipe is ribbed, so leaves and small twigs may become trapped and clog it. The slick pipe is smooth and is hard to clog. If it ever does stop up, you can simply run a sewer tape through it.

■ Put all the pipe together and connect it to the downspout. Set it on top of the ground so you can mark the outline of the pipe. This shows you exactly where you need to dig your trench.

■ While trenching, make sure the spot where the water will exit the pipe is lower than the spot where it enters the pipe from the downspout. One quarter inch of slope per foot should allow the water to run quickly through the pipe.

■ Now set the pipe in the trench, which should be deep enough for the pipe to be completely buried. Make sure the end of the pipe is positioned so that the water will flow away from your house.

■ You may want to glue the joints together, but it's really not necessary if they fit snugly.

■ Finally, cover the pipe with soil. A large stone may be set on top of the end of the pipe to hide it. 🌱

COLOR CORRECTION

A long time ago everyone decided all downspouts should be white. Now times are changing and so are the colors. Downspouts serve an important purpose but don't need to stand out.

If you are considering putting up gutters and downspouts remember that they are now available in a wide range of colors. Choose one that blends with your house.

Or paint existing downspouts the same color as your house.

Even if you and your neighbor are friendly, there's nothing wrong with a little privacy

Colorful crepe myrtles separate a pair of driveways without blocking the views.

If you're trying to decide between a fence or a hedge, planting has one advantage over building: Plants grow, fences don't. Save money by starting off with small trees or shrubs that will form a dense wall of foliage when mature.

When choosing plants, it's important to know which are evergreen and which are deciduous. Evergreen plants keep their leaves through winter. Deciduous plants lose all their leaves during dormancy and stay bare until spring. You will probably want to select evergreen plants so the view you want to hide isn't revealed during cold months. However, even fast-growing deciduous trees will

EVERGREEN TREES

Common Name	Botanical Name	Mature Height	Range
American holly	*Ilex opaca*	20-30 feet	AS
Canadian hemlock	*Tsuga canadensis*	50-70 feet	US, MS
*Eastern red cedar	*Juniperus virginiana*	30-40 feet	US, MS, LS
Foster's holly	*Ilex x attenuata* Fosteri	15-20 feet	AS
*Leyland cypress	*Cupressocyparis leylandii*	60-70 feet	US, MS, LS
*loquat	*Eriobotrya japonica*	15-20 feet	LS, CS
lusterleaf holly	*Ilex latifolia*	20-30 feet	MS, LS, CS
*Southern red cedar	*Juniperus silicicola*	20-30 feet	CS

EVERGREEN SHRUBS

Common Name	Botanical Name	Mature Height	Range
Burford holly	*Ilex cornuta* Burfordii	10-12 feet	AS
*cleyera	*Cleyera japonica*	6-8 feet	MS, LS, CS
Fortunes osmanthus	*Osmanthus x fortunei*	12-15 feet	MS, LS, CS
Japanese anise	*Illicium anisatum*	10-12 feet	MS, LS, CS
Nellie R. Stevens holly	*Ilex x Nellie R. Stevens*	15-20 feet	AS
*oleander	*Nerium oleander*	10-12 feet	CS

RAPID-GROWING DECIDUOUS TREES

Common Name	Botanical Name	Mature Height	Range
bald cypress	*Taxodium distichum*	50-60 feet	AS
chaste tree	*Vitex agnus-castus*	10-15 feet	LS, CS
crepe myrtle	*Lagerstroemia indica*	20-25 feet	MS, LS, CS
Eastern redbud	*Cercis canadensis*	20-25 feet	AS
river birch	*Betula nigra*	30-40 feet	AS
sycamore	*Platanus occidentalis*	60-70 feet	AS
Yoshino cherry	*Prunus yedoensis*	20-25 feet	US, MS, LS

* rapid growing; AS=All South, CS=Coastal South, LS=Lower South, MS=Middle South, US=Upper South

Bottom: A row of Leyland cypress marching down the hill blocks year-round views of a tall house next door.

Below: Foster's hollies form a neat screen of green.

DESIGN: PAT LEA, SIGNAL MOUNTAIN, TENNESSEE

go a long way toward establishing a sense of separation between areas. Refer to the chart above for those plants that will do well in your area. When choosing, keep in mind the plant's mature height.

One trick to make your screen look thicker faster is to set your plants in a zigzag pattern. This technique costs less than planting a double row of trees or shrubs and is more effective than a single straight-line row. Start by setting plants in a row, then pull every other one forward by one-half the distance between plants. Allow them to grow together so they touch, forming a pleasing wall of green.

(For sources see pages 250–251.)

Clueless in the flowerbed

With diminutive Little Miss Muffet daisies in front and taller heliopsis in back, this bed is arranged like steps on a stair.

A new flower garden is the proverbial blank page. Anything is possible, and that is the problem. Where do you begin? Start with what you like.

Choose your favorite color or color combinations. Remember, you don't have to grow everything. It's like planning a meal. You decide on the main dish, and then everything else is chosen to go along with it. If creating a color scheme is intimidating, use only one. Some of the most effective gardens are a single color.

Given a color scheme, **make a list of the perennials and annuals that will grow** in your area. Then consider the sun and soil, and strike the ones that are not adapted to the growing conditions in your garden.

The first rule of thumb is to **arrange your plants like a choir**—short in front, medium in the middle, and tall in back. The second rule is to **use a minimum of three plants of any type** to make a clump or pod. But feel free to plant more than three to make a sweep of color.

Place groups of plants that look good together next to each other. Plants complement each other in many ways. Perhaps they bloom at the same time in harmonious colors. Maybe they bloom at different times, giving you color over a longer period. One might be

Rose verbena adds bright color to the front of a bed.

The tall, graceful foliage of maiden grass makes it an excellent choice for the back of the bed.

A favorite in many borders, purple coneflower is easily grown from seed.

upright while the other is trailing, or one has a V-shaped form that is interesting next to a round mound.

If your perennials play out, **fill in with annuals** to carry the color through the summer. With the long growing season in the South, gardeners rely on annuals to get them through the summer when the spring perennials fade and the fall ones have yet to begin.

GET THE HEIGHT RIGHT

The perennials in the chart at right are all sun-loving, but they give you a place to start. Visualize how different plants with different heights can be placed for greatest impact. If you are surprised by a plant's size, just wait until fall and move it to a better spot.

(For sources see pages 250–251.)

TALL: BACK OF THE BORDER

maiden grass *(Miscanthus sinensis Gracillimus)*

cutleaf coneflower *(Rudbeckia laciniata)*

swamp sunflower *(Helianthus angustifolius)*

MEDIUM: ON MIDDLE GROUND

rough heliopsis *(Heliopsis scabra)*

purple coneflower *(Echinacea purpurea)*

Russian sage *(Perovskia atriplicifolia)*

SHORT: DOWN IN FRONT

rose verbena *(Verbena canadensis)*

dwarf-eared coreopsis *(Coreopsis auriculata Nana)*

Cheddar pinks *(Dianthus gratianopolitanus)*

Why your bulbs won't bloom

Nothing proclaims the arrival of spring like the sunny trumpets of daffodils. So it is disappointing when they don't bloom. You planted them a few years ago, and their leaves are there. Why aren't they flowering?

The most common reason that daffodils cease flowering is that the bulbs have become too crowded. They need to be lifted, divided, and replanted.

Too crowded. Daffodils reproduce by dividing and making new bulbs. That's why you often see a slender adolescent bulb attached to a large one when you buy them. But after several years, a single bulb can become an entire colony, with bulbs growing on the shoulders of other ones. None have enough moisture or nutrients to produce a flowerbud, however. **Solution:** Lift and divide them.

Insufficient sun. If planted in the dark recesses of your garden, your daffodils will grow weaker each season until they no longer have the stored energy to develop a flowerbud. **Solution:** Dig them up and move them to a bed where they get about six hours of sunshine each day.

Too warm. If you have had an unusually mild winter or you live in the Deep South where the only sure bet is planting paperwhite narcissus, such as Ziva or Galilee, your bulbs may not have had enough cold weather to break dormancy. **Solution:** Purchase precooled bulbs, or plant your bulbs in containers where they will be more exposed to any cold weather you get.

Foliage damage. If the leaves were removed prematurely, either by a late freeze or an impatient gardener, the bulbs cannot replenish their energy reserves for the following season. They may have enough left to grow leaves, but flowering will have to wait until they gain strength. **Solution:** Fertilize bulb beds from late fall to early spring with a slow-release fertilizer, such as 9-9-6, at the rate recommended on the package. Then let the foliage remain until it begins to yellow and flop over. ❧

TIRED TULIPS

Tulips rarely bloom a second time in most of the South because our weather gets too hot before the foliage has time to mature. Treat them as annuals, and plan to discard them, bulbs and all, after they have flowered.

Don't settle for scraggly azaleas

Shaping your azaleas is like getting a good haircut; the improvement is noticeable but the amount removed isn't. With a little attention, your plants will be as pretty as a picture. Artful pruning can get these shrubs in shape and keep them that way.

There's nothing lovelier than our region's trademark plant in full bloom.

If you trim azaleas during the wrong season, you will cut off next year's blossoms. That's because azaleas bloom on old wood, so they produce flowerbuds on last year's growth. You won't hurt the plant by pruning during warm months, but if you want flowers, hide your clippers after spring. The best time to trim azaleas is just after they've finished blooming.

Never prune azaleas with electric shears. Hand pruners are essential for doing the job right. If your shrubs haven't been shaped for a while, they've probably grown long woody stalks with clusters of foliage at the tips. Reach inside the plant to cut these stalks off where they join each branch. Not only will all cuts be hidden by surrounding foliage, but this technique also allows sunlight to penetrate to the center of the plant, encouraging new growth and flowers. (Flat-topping your azalea by trimming only the ends of branches results in dense twiggy growth with sparse foliage.)

Though you may end up with an alarmingly large pile of cut-off stalks, don't worry. Your azaleas won't look like they've just been butchered. That's because this pruning method allows the shrubs to maintain their natural, airy shape. ✿

CHOOSE THE RIGHT TOOL
Small pruners are fine for trimming pencil-width stems, but long-handled loppers are the tool of choice when cutting branches ½ inch to 1½ inches in diameter. The handles provide the leverage needed to make clean cuts.

If you see pale, fuzzy buds curled tight on the tips of branches, it's too late to prune azaleas without cutting off next year's flowers.

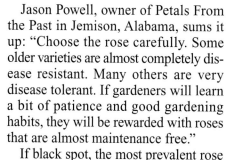
Buff Beauty

There's not a chemical in sight, and everything's coming up roses

Zéphirine Drouhin

No other flower evokes the emotional and covetous response like the rose. Gardeners are also well versed in the amount of work and spraying needed to raise long-stemmed regal blooms. But there is a way to have roses and not become a chemical warrior.

Climbing Pinkie

Jason Powell, owner of Petals From the Past in Jemison, Alabama, sums it up: "Choose the rose carefully. Some older varieties are almost completely disease resistant. Many others are very disease tolerant. If gardeners will learn a bit of patience and good gardening habits, they will be rewarded with roses that are almost maintenance free."

If black spot, the most prevalent rose disease, does occur, it will probably peak during the spring months. This is when evenings are still cool and moisture is high in the garden. Once the weather warms and rains diminish, many antique roses and some modern ones will shed diseased leaves and flush with new, stronger growth that is free of black spot. The secret is to be patient. Keep your roses well nourished and remove all diseased leaves that have fallen to the ground. In due time, black spot will vanish or greatly diminish.

There are other fringe benefits from planting antique roses. Many have a fragrance that will bring back memories of childhood. Some types bloom in clusters; one cut stem will give you an instant bouquet in a vase. Jason suggests that if you're limited on space, plant a Marie Pavié in a container. It is deliciously fragrant, blooms all summer, and stays well contained. ❧

(For sources see pages 250–251.)

Right: New Dawn is a vigorous climbing rose that blooms profusely in the spring.

The Southern Gardener section was written by Linda C. Askey, Steve Bender, Jo Kellum (coordinator), Ellen Riley, and Charlie Thigpen, with photography by Jean Allsopp, Van Chaplin, and Tina Cornett. Graphic design by Craig Smith.

Art From Your Garden

You can easily simulate a framed book of botanicals that's open for decoration and display. Press pansies fresh from the garden, and glue them to pages cut from watercolor paper. Frame the flowers in a shadow box you've lined with colorful mat board, and use a strip of ribbon as a bookmark.

Ask a frame shop to assemble a shadow box about 1½ inches deep. Choose mat board in a complementary shade and have it cut to fit inside the frame; the mat board's sides should be cut so that they fold up against the inside edges of the wooden frame. Purchase the materials you'll need to finish the framing at home, or return the project to the frame shop for completion.

Julia H. Thomason

STEP 1:
PLACE a sheet of cardboard inside a flower press; then add blotting paper and a layer of pansies. Cover flowers with blotting paper and cardboard. Continue sandwiching pansies between paper and cardboard. Replace top of flower press, and tighten screw. (An alternative is to press pansies in a telephone book until they are dry.)

STEP 2:
REMOVE mat from shadow box. Glue larger sheet of watercolor paper to center of mat. Fold smaller piece of paper in half, glue 1 inch of ribbon to underside of fold, and pull remaining ribbon to front. Glue fold to center of watercolor sheet, and press it down until glue dries. Glue short edges of paper in place, lifting them in the center like curved book pages. Remove dried pansies from flower press or telephone book. Apply glue to flowers one at a time, and arrange them on watercolor paper.

STEP 3:
INSERT glass into shadow box, add mat with attached watercolor paper and flowers, and insert cardboard backing and brads. Seal frame by gluing kraft paper to back; insert screw eyes, and add picture wire. Hang or prop your creation. ◇

TOOLS & MATERIALS

flower press with cardboard and blotting paper or telephone book

pansies

22- x 16-inch shadow box frame with glass, mat, and cardboard backing cut to fit

glue stick

large sheet of textured watercolor paper, cut into one 19- x 13-inch piece and one 18- x 11-inch piece

13-inch-long piece of 1-inch-wide ribbon

brads

kraft paper

screw eyes

picture wire

A shadow box is an elegant way to present dried pansies; they're glued to paper for the effect of an old flower book.

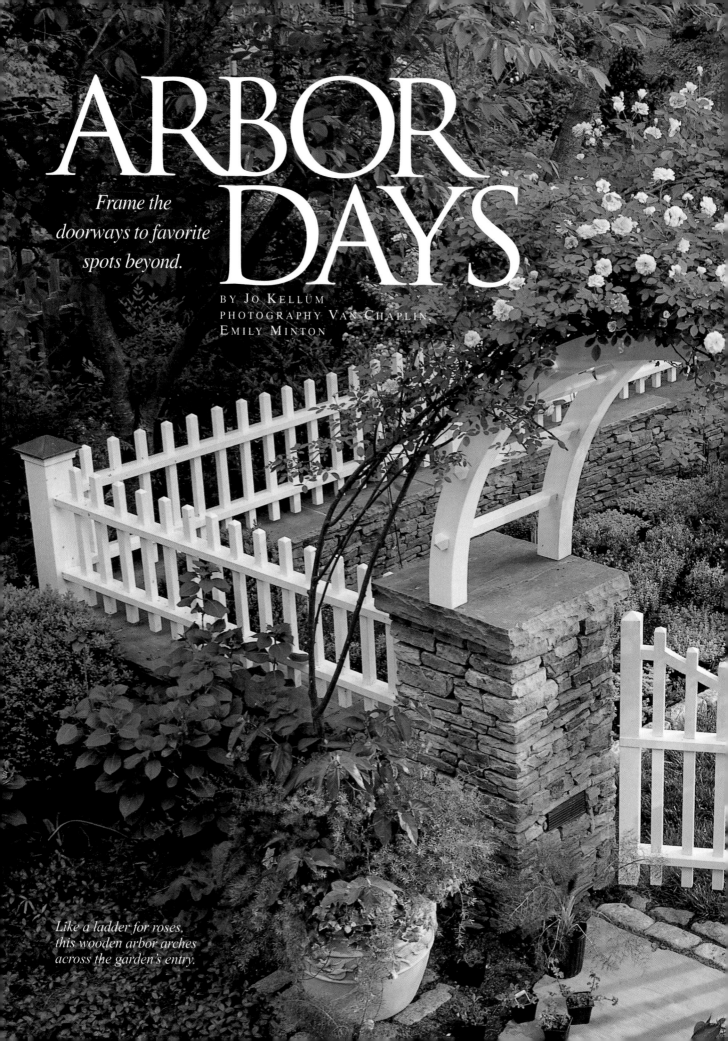

ARBOR DAYS

Frame the doorways to favorite spots beyond.

BY JO KELLUM
PHOTOGRAPHY VAN CHAPLIN,
EMILY MINTON

Like a ladder for roses, this wooden arbor arches across the garden's entry.

OWNERS: PAT AND TED PLOMGREN, ATLANTA / DESIGN: JEREMY SMEARMAN

Few among us can resist the power of a glimpse. Entirety cannot compete with the torn corner of a birthday package, a peek at a diary page, or a keyhole view into some enticing garden spot.

Put the allure of fleeting views to work for you. A bench is just a bench until it's seen through a vine-covered arbor; then it becomes a postcard-perfect destination. From simple peaked structures to more elaborate arches, arbors add the frame to living pictures.

Build an arbor to mark an invisible doorway connecting one garden spot to another. Be sure to include a worthy view. The focus of attention should beckon,

DESIGN: GERRY RENFROE, NEW MARKET, ALABAMA

Only 5 years old, this cherry laurel hedge offers passage through a wall of green. A shrub was omitted at planting to create the opening.

(Above) *A metal arbor wreathed in green arches above this garden gate.*

(Above, right) *The architectural lines of this arbor add an unexpected accent. The two-post design keeps construction simple.*

(Right, inset) *Split fence rails form a simple peaked arbor with rustic charm.*

leading you through the arbor and encouraging you to follow a curving walk, enter an intriguing door, or visit a favorite sitting spot.

Remember to turn around and look behind you; gardens are rarely seen in only one direction. The addition of trees, shrubs, or fencing to screen unwanted sights, and the careful placement of an accent plant or sculpture piece can make the arbor effective both coming and going.

Or, skip the structure and grow your own passageway with a peekaboo hedge.

Plant rapid-growing shrubs to form a hedgerow, strategically omitting one or two plants. While the hedge grows, prune as needed to shape the opening. Allow foliage to grow together as shrubs reach an overhead height. You may want to gently tie branch tips together to encourage the top of the arch to fill in. Good choices include cherry laurel, waxleaf ligustrum, wax myrtle, elaeagnus, Florida anise, and soft-leaved hollies such as upright yaupon and Burford. ◇

OVER-THE-TOP IDEAS

■ If you've got a problem with guests arriving through the family entrance, use an arbor to direct them to the formal entrance.

■ Don't let the sky be the limit. Vast exterior spaces can be over-whelming and uncomfortable. Add overhead structures to create people-size garden doorways.

■ Archways and arbors can make a small garden seem larger. Position the structure at the end of an entry corridor lined with trees, tall shrubs, or fencing. That way visitors must first pass through a confined space. In comparison, the garden beyond will appear bigger.

Flowering dogwoods (See pages 90–93.)

April

*Give vines
your support,
and raise your
garden off the
ground.*

High Stakes

BY CHARLIE THIGPEN
PHOTOGRAPHY VAN CHAPLIN

When the stakes are high, don't let your plants down. Stakes don't have to be poles stuck in the ground. We found morning glories gobbling up a brick wall, moonflowers stretching on a viny arch, and Marguarita sweet potato vine forming a lime-green tunnel over a garden gate. Plants can be trained to grow almost anywhere.

With a little assistance, some plants will twist and twine their way above the garden, creating a cloudlike effect. A vine's free-flowing form adds a loose element to an otherwise stuffy garden. It can also be used to disguise or hide an unattractive structure.

In most landscapes, you look down at the flowers, but with vines you can have flowers at eye level and even overhead. Find a place in your garden where vertical climbers can rise. Here are a few easy vines that drape the Southern landscape and are just waiting to take your garden up a notch.

■ Morning glory *(Ipomoea purpurea)* is a fast-growing annual vine that can be a nuisance. It grows like kudzu and reseeds with abandon. But because of its self-sufficient nature, it's also a favorite of gardeners. This vine comes in many colors, is simple to grow from seed, and can cover an arbor in the blink of an eye. Each morning, pointed, swollen buds twist open, turning into

These morning glories flourish on a support of fishing line that runs from nail to nail.

Good Old Daisies

There's nothing pretentious about daisies. You've loved these cheerful, common flowers ever since you learned to draw them in kindergarten. Perhaps it's because daisies grow in crayon colors: yellow centers ringed with white petals on plain green stems.

Shasta daisies *(Chrysanthemum maximum)* are the ones you probably remember from childhood. It's easy to add them to your own garden. Start with seeds or transplants in spring or fall. Autumn planting has the advantage of establishing root systems before flowering. Each 4-inch transplant you set out in fall will produce, at a fraction of the cost, roughly the same amount of blooms as a 1-gallon plant purchased in spring. But don't fret if you waited until spring to go daisy crazy; plants started now will continue to grow all year. If you leave spent flowers on their stems instead of trimming brown seedheads, your daisies will reseed.

Daisies are perennial, so consider your patch an ongoing addition to the garden. Dig up large clumps of them every other year around October, and cut roots apart to divide them. This will keep crowded roots from smothering each other and will offset the natural decline that occurs after two to three years. Set divisions 10 to 12 inches apart in full sun, or share them with friends. You can also dig seedlings from beneath parent plants in fall and replant them. Seeds purchased in packets may be sown in fall or spring.

AT A GLANCE

Size: 10 to 24 inches high
Light: full sun
Soil: moderately fertile, well drained
Range: All South
Comments: great cut flowers
Expect to pay: from $2 for a 4-inch pot to $7 for a 1-gallon container

Bed down Shastas for winter by tucking mulch around each plant, taking care not to cover leaves. The rosettes of foliage stay green year-round in much of the South. Alaska is a selection named for its tolerance for icy weather; this 2-foot beauty produces 2-inch flowers nonstop for at least a month in the spring and sporadically until cold weather returns. For a shorter Shasta, try Snow Lady, a hybrid measuring 10 to 12 inches high. Give plants a good drink of water during summer's dog days.

Shasta daisies will reward you with bright bouquets filled with heart-warming blooms. *Jo Kellum*

The Antique Rose Emporium in Brenham, Texas, collected Shasta daisies from an old homestead to start its patch.

Each spring, flowering almonds grace the garden of Margaret Sanders in Columbus, Mississippi. She dug them out from under an old fig tree years ago and says they thrive wherever she puts them.

Remembering Flowering Almond

Back in my college days, when I knew absolutely everything, I was sure that anyone who grew flowering almond must be an out-and-out boob. Why else would someone sacrifice their valuable garden space to a deciduous shrub that blooms just two weeks a year?

Now that I'm older and know much less than I once did, I have discovered the answer nevertheless. It has nothing to do with multiseason interest, design theory, or efficient use of space. It has to do with memories.

For you see, flowering almond *(Prunus glandulosa)* is one of those tough, old stalwarts our mothers grew

> ## AT A GLANCE
> **Size:** 3 to 5 feet tall and wide
> **Light:** full sun
> **Soil:** fertile, well drained
> **Pests:** none serious
> **Prune:** immediately after flowering in spring
> **Propagation:** division, cuttings
> **Range:** Upper, Middle, Lower, Coastal South
> **Expect to pay:** about $10

by the front porch, beside the wire fence, or in some out-of-the-way corner out back. For 50 weeks a year, it offered little charm. But then in early spring, it mingled its pink pompon blossoms with those of the forsythia, grape hyacinths, and spirea. Although the show was short-lived, the memory lasts forever.

Native to Japan and China, flowering almond grows into an open, rounded shrub 3 to 5 feet tall and wide. Blooms appear before the leaves in March or April and may be single or double, pink or white. Reports have it that the single forms set tiny, red fruits. But no one I know has seen this, probably because almost

everyone grows the doubles. Given full sun and fertile, well-drained soil, the shrub will survive for decades with little care. But to keep it from becoming straggly over the years, cut a few of the old, woody stalks to the ground every spring after they bloom.

If you have a hankering for flowering almond, visit your garden center soon. Most places don't keep it in stock after the springtime planting hysteria subsides. Don't buy just one, buy three or four—flowering almond always looks better planted en masse.

But be warned—inevitably some recent horticulture grad will observe your planting, shove a degree in your face, and question your taste. Don't flinch. Just smile in silence and note how insightful you are now that you know much less than before.

Steve Bender

Planted in a Pool

Sometimes there's just no room to garden. If a balcony or terrace is the majority of your outdoor space, or if you want to introduce a little green to any unplanted area, consider a using a cast-concrete pool for a miniature garden.

Because these pools are made to accommodate plumbing, there are holes in the bottom that allow for drainage. If the holes are so large that soil will wash out, partially cover them with a piece of broken terra-cotta pot. Fill the pool with a good quality potting soil, one that is fairly coarse so it will last several years.

Then consider the area where your pool garden will be placed. Will it have sun or shade? Do you want a spring, summer, fall, or all-season garden? Will you see it up close or in passing? Answers to these questions will determine what you choose to plant.

The pool garden shown here relies on shade-loving plants, giving it a foundation of foliage that is attractive all season long. Flowers come and go. The planting is highly detailed so it is interesting to look down upon at close range.

Like furnishing a dollhouse with miniature tables and chairs, planting a pool garden requires scaled-down thinking. The ground cover is a combination of moss and the dainty, diminutive *Lysimachia japonica* Minutissima. Shade-loving and growing all of a half-inch tall, it is an ideal choice. It even sports tiny yellow flowers in late spring.

Pushing through the blanket of green are miniature hostas (that flower in their season), dwarf crested iris *(Iris cristata)*, violas, Itsy-Bitsy English ivy, blue phlox *(Phlox divaricata),* and foamflower *(Tiarella wherryi).*

If space allows, repeat the showiest plants in the surrounding beds to tie it all together.   *Linda C. Askey*

Editor's note: Deep bird baths also make good containers for bog plants. ◇

PHOTOGRAPHS: VAN CHAPLIN

A cast-concrete pool can be pressed into service as a planter. This shade-loving combination includes (from top left) blue phlox, miniature hostas with golden and variegated foliage, and dwarf crested iris. In the pool, the iris are safe from hungry voles that may devour them in garden beds.

Grow for Freshness

Each spring, small rectangular and square vegetable gardens pop up in quiltlike patterns in backyards all across the South. Many people are following in their parents' and grandparents' footsteps. But even if your family didn't garden, give it a try. You may be starting a new tradition.

Last spring I tilled a 15- x 25-foot area. Next I added leaf mold and sand to the clay soil and tilled the bed until the soil was loose. Then I removed all the rocks. After planting and pampering I was amazed at how this small patch of earth provided my family and friends with so many tasty meals. As our refrigerator filled, I began asking my friends if they would like some vegetables. I was surprised by their excited reactions. People not only wanted the vegetables—they treated them as treasures. This produce wouldn't have cost much if they had bought it at the grocery store, but people appreciate the taste of freshly harvested vegetables.

I planted five rows 25 feet in length. The first row, starting on the back side of the garden, consisted of okra. The second row had tomatoes. The third contained bush beans and eggplant, while the fourth row had sweet banana and bell peppers. The last row held yellow and zucchini squash. All of these vegetables are simple to grow. Cucumbers, pole beans, green onions, and peas are a few others that are easy to grow and good for the beginner's spring garden.

Vegetable gardening is not hard; it just takes a little time and effort. You do have to tend to your plot every couple of days just to see how things are growing. By observing the garden regularly, you're able to detect problems, such as bug damage or the spread of fungus or disease, and correct them before they get out of hand. When you encounter these problems you can go to books, a county Extension agent, or a reputable garden center to find solutions.

Remember, gardening does require a little work. Tilling and adding leaf mold or sand to your soil can be physically challenging. Then as your garden grows, you'll be weeding and watering. Don't forget, the bigger the garden the more work involved. Start small, and—as your knowledge and interest increase—expand your garden.

Choose a good location. Your site must receive at least six to eight hours of full sun. Check the condition of the soil. Dark, rich, loose soil will need little work, while rocky clay soil will need a great deal of amending and tilling. If the site you choose stays damp, you will have to make a raised bed because vegetables need good drainage.

This year don't just harvest vegetables from the produce aisle at the supermarket. Till some soil and plant your own. You'll get a good workout, you'll learn, and you'll taste the freshness.

Charlie Thigpen

When planting vegetables, make sure taller plants, such as okra and tomatoes, are on the back side where they won't shade the others.

PHOTOGRAPHS: VAN CHAPLIN

Margaret's Secret Garden

Margaret Deimling's secret garden isn't around back. It's right in front of the house. But to see it, you have to walk a few steps up the driveway. It's all part of an ingenious solution to a common parking problem.

Her previous narrow driveway ran straight into the garage under the house. Cars that pulled in couldn't turn around—they had to slowly back out. So Atlanta landscape architect Bill Smith cut into the slope in front of the house and added a turnaround and guest parking area. Then he designed a small flower garden that's the first thing Margaret sees when she opens her front door.

But you can't see this sunken garden from the street. It sits about 4 feet below the front lawn. Only the top of a brick retaining wall hints at its presence—that and the blooms of New Dawn roses peeking over the wall in spring.

Detail is everything in a garden this small. Bill didn't miss a trick.

Here are some of the highlights.
- At the head of the turnaround the brick landing ties together the retaining walls and new front steps.
- The Chippendale bench matches the porch railing. It also acts as a focal point when you look down from the top of the steps.
- Dyed concrete in the driveway complements the colors of the house while also reducing glare.

- A strong backbone of evergreen shrubs and ground covers lends year-round visual interest.

Margaret's secret garden is such a hit with her neighbors that it won't be a secret long. "We live in a neighborhood where people walk a lot," she says. "And whenever I'm out in the yard, people always stop and tell me how much they love to look at the flowers." *Steve Bender*

BEFORE

Cutting into the slope in front of the house allowed the construction of a new turnaround and guest parking area, plus a sunken garden hidden from the street.

Imagine this much privacy without even a fence. Only the roses are visible from the street beyond. The Chippendale bench repeats the look of the porch railing.

Tips On Iris

If the beautiful iris in the gardens of Marie Caillet and Shirley Welch on page 86 have you itching to try these plants, here are some easy guidelines.

Louisiana iris are well adapted to the Upper, Middle, Lower, and Coastal South. They prefer an acid to neutral pH. Almost any soil—boggy or well drained—is fine, but amend heavy clay or sandy soil with organic matter.

If you receive rhizomes (fleshy roots) through the mail, soak them in water overnight before planting. The garden should receive at least a half-day of sun and preferably a full day. Place each rhizome 1 inch deep in the ground; then cover the soil surface with an inch of mulch. Keep the soil moist. Rhizomes that dry out in summer may not bloom the next spring. Louisianas are heavy feeders. Sprinkle a handful of azalea and camellia fertilizer around each plant in March and September. You can also feed them with a water-soluble, acid-forming fertilizer, such as Miracid, just before and after they bloom.

Bearded iris are suited to the Upper, Middle, and Lower South. They accept moderately acid to moderately alkaline soil. Excellent drainage is a must. Add organic matter to the soil before planting.

Choose a sunny location. Plant the rhizomes shallowly, so that the tops of the fleshy roots are even with or just protruding above the soil surface. In the Lower South, place a half-inch of light mulch atop the rhizomes to prevent sun scald. Keep the soil moist during periods of active growth; it's okay for the soil to go fairly dry during summer, however. Sprinkle a handful of Holland Bulb Booster 9-9-6 around each plant in spring. Then feed each plant with water-soluble fertilizer just before and after it blooms. ◆

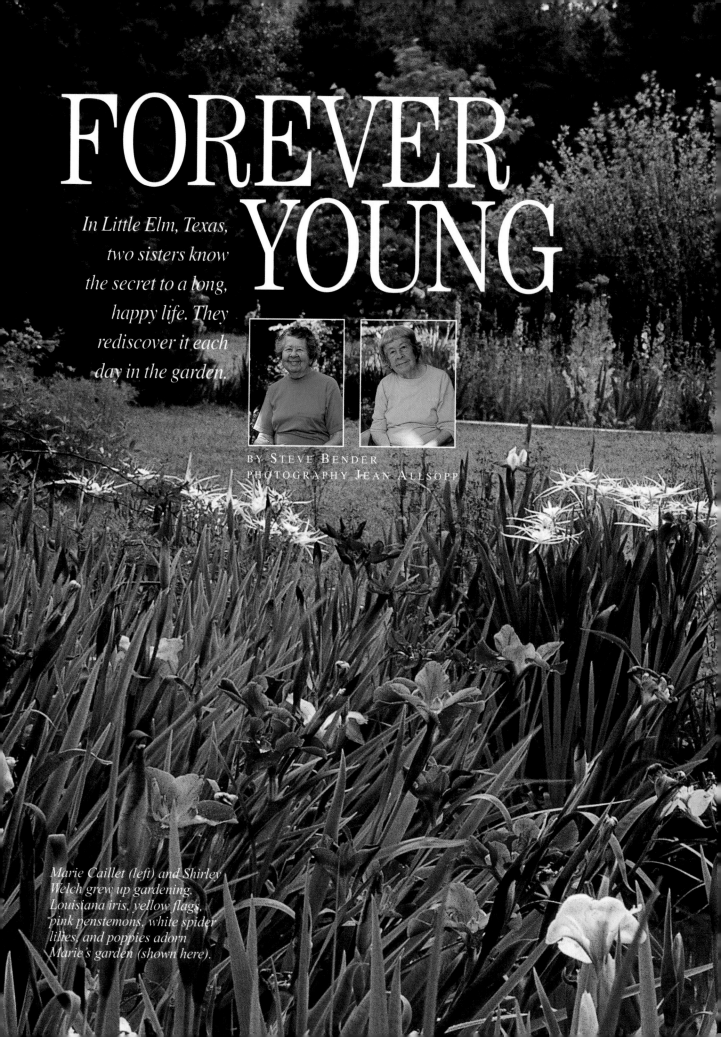

FOREVER YOUNG

In Little Elm, Texas, two sisters know the secret to a long, happy life. They rediscover it each day in the garden.

BY STEVE BENDER
PHOTOGRAPHY JEAN ALLSOPP

Marie Caillet (left) and Shirley Welch grew up gardening. Louisiana iris, yellow flags, pink penstemons, white spider lilies, and poppies adorn Marie's garden (shown here).

"I feel sorry for people who do not like to grow things and get their hands dirty," Shirley Welch says earnestly. "I think it was intended for us to keep our hands and bodies close to the earth."

Today, as she does almost every day, Shirley will have lunch with her sister, Marie Caillet (pronounced Cal-YAY), who lives across the quiet country lane that separates their yards. They'll talk about the usual things—who called this morning, which iris beds need digging, and how long it took Marie to drive 600 miles to New Orleans and back. There's nothing really notable about this, until you consider that Marie is 82. Shirley is 94. They've been gardening together on the shores of Lewisville Lake, 45 minutes north of Dallas, for the last 30 years.

The sisters attribute their interest in plants to French ancestors who arrived in Texas in 1855 and counted botanists among their ranks. Marie and Shirley's mother, Laura, inherited the "green gene" and started her own nursery at their home on Lover's Lane in Dallas in the late 1920s. She raised bearded iris and sold them for up to a dollar apiece, earning enough money to buy her first car. "Bearded iris were very popular," recalls Marie,

"but many were introduced at a high price. I remember once our mother paid $25 for one. That was a lot of money back then. She put a little fence around it."

The girls routinely helped weed and water the garden. "We lived in the country and didn't have a lot of close neighbors or playmates," remembers Shirley. "So our mother and father saw to it that we enjoyed the outdoors. Gardening wasn't a job for us. We had fun."

Reaching adulthood, the sisters went into teaching. Shirley served as an elementary school principal for 23 years.

She was so popular with her students that they addressed her as "Aunt Shirley." She married Clyde Welch (who died five years ago) and moved to her present home on family land in 1960. Marie taught at the University of Southwestern Louisiana in Lafayette for 33 years. She retired in 1972 and moved next door to her older sister.

Special irises from Marie's former garden accompanied her. They weren't bearded iris, which disliked the Louisiana climate. Instead, they were Louisiana iris, hybrids of five species of iris native to the South. Louisianas bloomed in every color of the rainbow. Unlike the beardeds, they relished hot, steamy weather and soggy soil. Few people knew about them, however.

Marie decided to change that. She helped found the Society for Louisiana Irises and co-authored a book, *The Louisiana Iris,* which has become a standard reference. She also planted hundreds of selections in her garden. Photographs of Marie's iris, gleaming like multicolored jewels above the inky water of her small pond, did more to popularize these plants than almost anything else. Scores of selections are now available. A blue one bears her name.

Shirley, however, stuck with the bearded iris that her parents had planted years ago. In fact, the only Louisiana iris she owns is Aunt Shirley, a huge, pink bicolor named for her. She explains the situation like this—she has the high ground and good drainage, which beardeds prefer; Marie has the low ground and the pond, just right for Louisianas. In spring, the spectacle of both gardens draws scads of visitors. "It's a good thing we're real sociable and love company," notes Shirley. "But that's how we've made some of our best friends."

(Top, left) *If forced to pick a favorite, Shirley might point to Beverly Sills, a wonderful coral-pink with an orange beard.*

(Bottom, left) *Unlike bearded iris, Louisianas like wet feet and steamy weather. One of Marie's favorites is purple Professor Ike.*

Contented iris multiply like the proverbial loaves and fishes. So if friends play their cards right, they will likely be granted an iris or two. "We have plenty to give away whenever people stop," says Shirley. "Marie scolds me and says there's a special time when bearded iris should be dug. But I just dig them anytime somebody comes by."

Nearly 95, Shirley has slowed a bit. Marie, meanwhile, buzzes from project to project. She's currently revising the Louisiana iris book, due out in late 1999 from Timber Press. She believes keeping mentally and physically active after retirement is key to a long, fruitful life.

"A lot of my friends have no hobbies, no outside interests, and they don't know what to do," she laments. "It's pitiful. I just went to a funeral last week of a lady who was younger than I am, and I'll bet she never walked any farther than from the house to the car."

Gardening may extend life, but it can't prolong it forever. Shirley and Marie find satisfaction in the fact that so many of their plants thrive in family and friends' gardens. Plants, like children, let gardeners glimpse immortality.

And who knows, perhaps many springs from now, someone in Texas will spy a pair of iris plants, vigorous and exuberant. Once again, Marie Caillet will bloom beside Aunt Shirley. ◇

Shirley prefers growing bearded iris on her higher ground. They multiply with abandon, so she has plenty to share.

For planting tips turn to page 85.

(For sources see pages 250–251.)

Blossoms of

BY STEVE BENDER
PHOTOGRAPHY
VAN CHAPLIN

the Heart

To Southerners, a dogwood is more than a tree. It's a symbol of hope, fidelity, friendship, and renewal.

Every spring, a Southerner's heart becomes a little crowded because a dogwood takes up half the space.

That Southerners love flowering dogwood *(Cornus florida)* was never more evident than when we asked our readers to send us remembrances and interesting facts about this native tree. Mail flooded in. Envelopes held photographs, short stories, and even a flower or two.

Talk about interesting facts. You know dogwood's reputation for being delicate and temperamental? Alice Pryor of Jefferson City, Tennessee, tells of her 50-year-old white dogwood broken off at the ground by careless construction workers. Not only did it live, the regrown tree now sports pink and white blooms!

In Winnsboro, Texas, 89-year-old Pete Forshee remembers splitting rails for fences as a boy. He used wedges and chisels made from dogwood. Only the wood of hickory is harder, heavier, and more durable. William Thomas of Oak Ridge, Tennessee, stresses the ecological importance of dogwoods. He says they serve as "calcium pumps" by absorbing large amounts of this nutrient from the subsoil, concentrating it in their leaves, then bestowing it to

the soil surface. When the leaves drop in fall, dogwoods feed their neighbors.

These trees enrich the spirit too. Paula Rogers of Chesterfield, Virginia, remembers two desolate years living in the Arizona desert. Finally, her family was called back to Virginia. On the drive home, white dogwoods laid out the welcome mat in Tennessee. "The dogwoods that lined the roads all the way back to Richmond . . . were my Southern sentinels," she writes. "They reminded me of all I had missed about the South: the refinement, the grace, the beauty, the glory of the spring. I knew I was back home."

Quite a few readers told us how dogwood blooms celebrated anniversaries. Jerry Bigner of Shreveport, Louisiana, recalls the letters her grandfather, a traveling salesman, sent to her grandmother. "He wrote, 'I'll be home to get you when the dogwoods are in bloom,' " she says. "And every year [he] would bring from the woods bouquets of dogwood as a reminder of his love." Their marriage, born on Easter Sunday, 1903, lasted 67 years.

For many, the cruciform blossoms of dogwood symbolize hope, renewal, and rebirth. Gelynda Underwood of Carthage, North Carolina, is one.

On July 11, 1995, she found a yearling dogwood, growing by the side of the road, that was due to be mowed down. She wanted to transplant it, but her husband warned it would surely die if dug in summer.

"[That] really shook me," she says. "You see, a year to the day had passed since our third child was born 15 weeks premature, and we were told then he would not live. Well, our miracle child did live, so I decided to plant [this dogwood] for him on his first birthday. After two weeks and lots of care, the tree was still alive, and we took Dillon's picture with his tree. I figure the tree should be around 3 years old this July, just like Dillon."

DEALING WITH DOGWOODS

Flowering dogwood will not grow in the Tropical South, unfortunately. Elsewhere, it needs moist, acid, well-drained soil. Full sun is fine, if the soil is deep and fertile. Otherwise, plant it beneath tall pines and hardwoods, so it receives afternoon shade. Be sure to water during summer droughts or the leaves will scorch badly. Watch out for anthracnose, a deadly disease that begins as purple-rimmed spots or tan blotches on leaves and flowers. To control it, apply Daconil 2787 once a week

Like clouds tethered to the ground, dogwoods adorn the South each spring. In full sun, they grow rounded and dense; in shade, they are open and airy.

(**Left**) *This pink specimen graces Louise Hammond's garden in Annapolis.* (**Above**) *Fall sees glorious color too: Leaves turn bright red and crimson before dropping.*

from the time the first blooms open until the leaves are fully expanded.

Most trees grow 15 to 25 feet tall and wide, but some get bigger, and in a few cases, a *lot* bigger. A dogwood in the yard of Margaret Thurmond in Charleston, Missouri, stands 37 feet high with a spread of 49 feet and a trunk circumference of 5 feet, 7 inches. It's the Missouri State Champion.

Nursery-grown dogwoods sometimes struggle to adjust to people's yards. Michael Murphy, a certified arborist in Beaufort, South Carolina, thinks he's discovered a remedy. He says that after inoculating the root zones of two dogwoods in a city planting with mycorrhiza— beneficial soil fungi that help roots absorb nutrients—the trees responded "with incredible results. In every aspect, they were superior to the other trees." How can you get mycorrhiza? Scoop up a jarful of woodsy soil beneath a natural stand of dogwoods. Add it to the soil mix when you plant your tree.

If you want to try growing dogwoods from seeds, follow the advice of Mary Coleman in Prescott, Arkansas. Gather berries in fall, scrape off the red pulp, and dry the seeds. Around December 15, plant the seeds atop the ground, covering them with pine straw or oak leaves; then lay wire screen atop that. Remove this covering in mid-March. Seedlings will sprout shortly. Mary, an active gardener in her nineties, has grown 18 dogwoods this way. ◇

(For sources see pages 250–251.)

Jacob's bean house (See pages 114–115.)

May

Checklist
for
May

EDITORS' NOTEBOOK

Friends, I bring to your attention the serious problem of daffodil abuse. No city or town is safe from its excesses. Your own family may include an abuser. We see the signs in late spring, when certain gardeners tire of daffodil foliage and start to "tidy" the garden. Some fold the leaves and secure them with rubber bands. Others go so far as to braid leaves into green ponytails. Chronic abusers claim they do no harm, but logic tells us otherwise. Folding and braiding leaves reduces photosynthesis and the storage of starches necessary for next spring's bloom. A better idea is to use the expanding foliage of companion plants, such as daylilies or tall ground covers, to hide daffodil leaves until they wither. Friends, if you know a daffodil abuser, you owe it to them to get help today. A bulb is a terrible thing to waste.

Steve Bender

☐ **Azaleas**—In Florida and other warm areas, some azaleas bloom again in the fall. Although the show is not as tremendous as in spring, it is enough to make you want these beauties for their surprise. Look for these selections: Happy Days, Red Ruffles, Gwenda, Higasa, Amaghasa, Duc de Rohan, Duchess of Cypress, and Fashion.

☐ **Cold damage**—Give those slow-to-sprout shrubs and perennials another month or two before you pull them out. And don't risk their tentative survival by digging them up to see how they're doing.

☐ **Lawns**—To encourage grass to grow in difficult areas, thin trees and remove lower limbs so that three to four hours of sunlight reach the turf. Select a shade-tolerant, warm-season grass such as St. Augustine or a cool-season blend. Mow grass about a half-inch taller than usual, and be sure to remove fallen leaves and debris promptly. If all else fails, redesign the area to utilize mulch or ground covers.

☐ **Mosquitoes**—When growing tropical plants outdoors, remember that bromeliads such as *Billbergia* species can collect enough water in their centers to act as breeding grounds for mosquitoes. Hang them from trees so they can't hold water as they do in the ground.

☐ **Support**—Tall-growing annuals and perennials that are top-heavy need to be staked before they fall over. These include foxgloves, delphiniums, lilies, and peonies. Use 6-foot stakes driven into the ground about 6 inches from the base of the stalk. Tie stalks to the stakes with strips of soft fabric. ▶

☐ **Tomatoes**—Keep plants evenly watered so they develop properly. Too little water followed by too much can cause fruit to crack. Mulch around the plants with 2 to 3 inches of compost, bark, or pine straw.

☐ **Roses**—It's not too late to plant container-grown roses. Remember, if you buy disease-tolerant selections, you don't have to spray at the first sign of black spot or mildew. Allow the plants to grow through the disease.

☐ **Summer bulbs**—As soon as all danger of frost has passed in the Middle and Upper South and the soil has begun to warm, set out bulbs of caladiums, callas, elephant's-ears, acidanthera, gladioli, cannas, dahlias, and tuberoses.

◀ **Vegetables**—In the Middle, Lower, and Coastal South, plant summer vegetables such as squash, cucumbers, tomatoes, peppers, Southern peas, okra, watermelons, and beans now. Add a row or two of sunflowers, zinnias, marigolds, or other favorite cut flowers to the vegetable garden for an abundance of fresh summer bouquets. In the Upper South, wait until the end of the month.

☐ **Vines**—Plant gourds, morning glories, hyacinth bean, moonflower, and cypress vine from seed or purchased plants. Allow at least 6 to 8 feet of sunny trellis, fence, or arbor area for each plant because they all grow large quickly. ▶

PRUNE

☐ **Bananas**—Thin crowded stalks to give plants the room they need to produce large banana clusters. Cut away suckers at the base as they appear, or divide them from the parent plant to transplant. For good production, leave at least 8 feet between bearing stalks.

☐ **Bulb foliage**—Spring-flowering bulbs need their foliage to mature and yellow before it's removed so that they will bloom again next spring. To help conceal the unattractive foliage, interplant bulbs with long-blooming annuals such as petunias, wax begonias, or marigolds.

☐ **Deadhead**—Remove spent flowers from pansies, snapdragons, stock, calendulas, and other spring-flowering annuals to extend their bloom season and keep the plants from getting leggy.

☐ **Magnolias**—Do not remove lower limbs if you can avoid it. Southern magnolia has two sins: Its shallow roots will not allow anything to grow beneath it, and the fallen leaves are notoriously slow to decay. Keep a skirt of branches close to the ground to hide both sins.

☐ **Roses**—Trim climbing roses as they complete their spring blooming season. Remove dead or weak wood from plants as needed. Shorten long, healthy canes by about one-third, and secure them to trellises, fences, or arbors with grass twine or other fasteners.

☐ **Shrubs**—Immediately after they flower, prune azaleas, forsythias, weigelas, quinces, and any other spring-flowering shrub. But remember, you don't have to prune unless you need to correct a plant's form, reduce its size, or cut out dead or diseased wood. Otherwise, enjoy these carefree characters.

☐ **Thyme**—Cut back leafless mats of creeping thyme stems to the point where new growth has sprouted. Fertilize with liquid 20-20-20 to encourage new growth.

CONTROL

☐ **Lawns**—Proper mowing height is the best weed control. A taller mowing height will also help your lawn survive dry weather.

FERTILIZE

☐ **Citrus**—In Lower South and Coastal areas, fertilize this month with a specially formulated citrus food containing iron and other minor elements. Rates vary according to brand, but in general apply about ½ pound of fertilizer per year of tree age. To control mites and scale on citrus, spray with an ultrafine oil such as SunSpray.

☐ **Houseplants**—Repot houseplants moved outdoors for summer in pots an inch or two larger in diameter. Or replace old soil with fresh in the original pot. Mix in a time-release fertilizer such as 18-18-18 for easier summer feeding. Ferns and other heavy feeders such as tropicals will appreciate a weekly dose of liquid food such as 20-20-20 too. ▶

☐ **Lawns**—Feed warm-season lawns, such as Zoysia, Bermuda, buffalo grass, and St. Augustine with 6 pounds of 16-4-8 or similar fertilizer per 1,000 square feet of lawn. Purchase a fertilizer that contains a slow-release formula so it doesn't release at one time and wash off with the first rain.

☐ **Mulch**—Apply composted pine bark, hay, dried grass clippings, or similar materials to flowerbeds and shrub borders to conserve moisture and reduce weed growth.

"More bang for the buck" was the philosophy behind this garden.

Blooming on a Budget

BY ELLEN RILEY
PHOTOGRAPHY VAN CHAPLIN

Sharon Whittington is a down-in-the-dirt gardener. "In my dreams, I see flowers everywhere," she says. She loves to work on a garden project from start to finish, all by herself. But, she's also busy—and on a budget. Sharon and her husband, Allen, have developed a plan for their landscape and tackle it one project at a time. The new garden was part of that plan.

DRAWING THE LINE

The Whittingtons wanted the shape of the new garden to complement the projects they had already completed. Thus, the arbor mirrors the arched shape of the front door, and the fence was placed with a gentle curve to make a welcoming frame for the new garden. By giving the front of the bed a curved edge, the appearance is casual and reflects the style of the house.

Sharon got out the hose and set to work. She placed it where the edge of the garden would be, then moved it around until the shape of the bed

BEFORE

was exactly as she wanted. Once the boundaries of the garden were determined, Sharon sprayed landscape paint to outline the space.

FROM SOD TO SOIL

"Over time, I've learned the difference between a fair garden and a great garden is the soil," says Sharon. "It's worth taking the time to do it right." First, she sprayed an

herbicide to kill the grass. In about two weeks the garden was ready to till. Using a spade, Sharon dug a shallow trench outlining the border. Then, she loosened the old turf with a garden fork. Sand and compost were raked over the surface of the garden to amend the soil. After running the tiller over the bed several times, she raked it smooth. It was ready to plant.

PLANT	PLACE IN GARDEN	LIGHT
1. Gold Star zinnia (*Zinnia angustifolia*)	front	sun
2. White Star zinnia (*Z. angustifolia*)	front	sun
3. purple heart (*Setcreasea pallida* Purple Heart)	front	sun
4. Mexican heather (*Cuphea hyssopifolia*)	front	sun
5. Powis Castle artemesia (*Artemesia* x Powis Castle)	middle	sun/part shade
6. Snow Nymph salvia (*Salvia coccinea*)	middle	sun
7. Medallion melampodium (*Melampodium* sp.)	middle	sun/part shade
8. coleus—sun-loving types	middle	sun/part shade
9. purple-leaved fountain grass (*Pennisetum setaceum* Rubrum)	middle	sun/part shade
10. butterfly bush (*Buddleia* sp.)	back	sun
11. spider flower (*Cleome spinosa*)	back	sun
12. giant alocasia (*Alocasia macrorrhiza*)	back	sun/part shade

Filled with annuals and perennials, the bed is overflowing with color that will last throughout the summer.

LOOKS LIKE A MILLION

Now Sharon was faced with a large, empty planting bed (22 feet long and 4 to 8 feet wide). "My biggest problem when I shop for plants is wanting it all," she confesses. "I have to go with something specific in mind." Her goal was to find maximum flower power for minimal cost.

Sharon first considered her garden's growing conditions. Most of the bed receives about six hours of direct sunlight, but it also curves under some trees at its western end. She needed flowers for full sun and partial shade. She also wanted continuous blooms from the time she planted until the first frost of fall.

She discovered a range of economical plants that grow big and bushy or provide nonstop flowers. See her shopping list below.

In addition, she wanted a few flowers for cutting. Globe amaranth *(Gomphrena globosa),* annual black-eyed Susans *(Rudbeckia hirta),* and Envy zinnias did the trick.

WEATHER OR NOT

Although her plant choices were excellent, the weather interfered. The annual black-eyed Susans and the Envy zinnias did not last the entire summer and had to be replaced. The globe amaranth never thrived and also had to be replaced.

As the summer progressed, the weather became more predictable. In midsummer, the butterfly bush began to bloom, and the Snow Nymph salvia filled out to add a light look to the garden. The spider flower bloomed, and Sharon's plan finally fell into place. ◇

First Sharon marked the bed line with paint. Then, she used herbicide to kill the grass within the bed, and dug a trench to outline the border.

Soil preparation is the key to a successful garden. To give her plants a good foundation, Sharon tilled in lots of sand and compost.

SHARON'S SHOPPING LIST

3 purple heart 4" pots; $1.95 each	$5.85
4 Mexican heather 4" pots; $2.95 each	11.80
4 Medallion melampodium packs of 3; 88 cents each	3.52
7 sun-loving coleus 4" pots; $1.95 each	13.65
7 globe amaranth packs of 3; 88 cents each	6.16
5 annual black-eyed Susans 1-gallon pots; $4.95 each	24.75
3 butterfly bush gallon pots; $4.95 each	14.85
2 Powis Castle artemesia 1-gallon pots; $4.95 each	9.90
10 Star zinnia packs of 3; 88 cents each	8.80
3 Snow Nymph salvia 4" pots; $2.95 each	8.85
1 flat Envy zinnia	9.95
3 purple-leaved fountain grass 1-gallon pots; $4.95 each	14.85
1 giant alocasia bulb	9.95
3 spider flower packs of 3; 88 cents each	2.64
Total:	**$145.52**

Sharon had saved a tropical blue plumbago from the summer before. She placed it in the back of the flower border on top of a turned-over pot. This was a no-cost bonus and a needed touch of blue for the garden.

Replacements:

4 globe amaranth 4" pots; $1.95 each	$7.80
5 annual black-eyed Susans 1-gallon pots; $4.95 each	24.75
1 flat annual zinnia	9.95
Total:	**$42.50**

Sharon placed all of the plants on top of the soil first. That made it easier to move them around until she had them just the way she wanted.

A Garden Winner

Yellow corydalis is about as well-known as the players on the NBA's Dallas Mavericks. But unlike that band of hapless hoopsters, this plant is truly a winner.

Before you can learn more about it, you have to learn to pronounce its name. All together now: ko-RID-a-lis. Very good. This newfound knowledge and sophistication is sure to dazzle your friends.

But yellow corydalis (*Corydalis lutea*) will probably impress them even more. Native to Europe, this engaging, little perennial does two things all gardeners love. First, it blooms in the shade, so it's a welcome addition to the woodland garden. Second, it blooms for a very long time. In the cooler reaches of the Upper and Middle South, corydalis may bloom all spring and summer. In warmer climes, it blooms from spring into early summer, then goes dormant during hot, dry weather.

Cheery, yellow blossoms, which look like tiny snapdragons, aren't its only selling point. Another is its finely cut foliage, which reminds you of columbine and maidenhair fern. The delicate leaves combine wonderfully with larger leaved plants, such as hostas, wild ginger (*Asarum canadense*), lily-of-the-valley (*Convallaria majalis*), lady's-mantle (*Alchemilla vulgaris*), and Lenten rose (*Helleborus orientalis*).

Once you get yellow corydalis going, it stays with you. Individual plants are somewhat short-lived, but seedlings come up all about. They prefer moist, well-drained soil that's rich in organic matter. Shield your plants from hot afternoon sun.

Yellow corydalis may not be able to dunk or rebound; then again, it won't cost you $10 million over 4 years. And you don't have to talk with an agent. *Steve Bender*

If you can't find corydalis at your local nursery, see pages 250–251 for sources.

YELLOW CORYDALIS
At a Glance

Size: grows 12 to 15 inches tall
Light: shade or partial shade
Soil: moist, well drained, lots of organic matter
Pests: none serious
Propagation: seedlings
Range: Upper, Middle, Lower South
Expect to pay: $7 to $8 for a 4-inch container

Yellow corydalis is a fine addition to the woodland border. Its ferny foliage blends well with the coarser leaves of hostas and ajuga. The bright yellow blossoms resemble tiny snapdragons. They appear all spring and summer in cooler parts of the South.

PHOTOGRAPHS: ALLEN ROKACH

Plant Collector's Paradise

BY STEVE BENDER
PHOTOGRAPHY ALLEN ROKACH

Conifers, shrubs, perennials, and ground covers blanket a boulder-strewn slope. The sheer variety provides year-round interest.

Those of us who love plants know the feeling all too well—you see a new plant, you just gotta have it, you bring it home, and then you ask, "Now where in the heck am I going to put it?"

That's the story behind this remarkable garden. Located near Baltimore, it contains hundreds of different plants—trees, shrubs, perennials, ornamental grasses, wildflowers, and ground covers—woven together on a hillside among footpaths of native stone. Despite its unnatural variety, it appears quite natural. And it all began because its owner has a hard time saying no.

The owner, who asked to remain anonymous, recalls that when she and her husband bought the property, there was no garden, save for a few existing trees. But both come from gardening families, so they quickly began amassing plants. Many arrived by mail. Others were acquired during car trips to the Northeast. Billed as family vacations, these outings often turned into hunting expeditions. "By the time we got back from New Hampshire and Connecticut," she admits, "the children would be literally surrounded by green."

Before long, coveys of conifers, lilies, and Japanese maples roosted on the hillside. To bring order and turn it into a coherent design, the owners contacted nurseryman and garden designer Kurt Bluemel of Baldwin, Maryland.

Kurt rearranged the collections with an eye toward the natural contours of the site. He also suggested dozens of new shrubs, grasses, and perennials. Today, this smorgasbord of contrasting foliage colors, sizes, and textures is fascinating to wander through in any season. Outcroppings, footpaths, and walls made of native stone hold it all together.

When asked about her favorite plants, the owner quickly cites needle-leaved conifers—dwarf Colorado blue spruce, blue atlas cedar, golden Hinoki false cypress, and

Keeping up with so many different plants is a challenge, but one the owners enjoy. "Gardening is so important to our lives, we can't even put it into words."

umbrella pine, to name a few. "They add structure and color to the garden year-round," she notes. "You can do spectacular things even in traditional borders by using conifers as backdrops and accents." She touts underappreciated shrubs, such as viburnums, witch hazels, and yellowtwig dogwood. She praises lilies as "totally fearless and self-sufficient." And she commends Japanese maples because "they're wonderful for small gardens; there are many different kinds, and they're all very beautiful."

A garden this diverse needs plenty of attention, but here the work is relished. "Gardening is very relaxing, and it's great exercise," she explains. "I love the mental challenge of learning how to grow new plants. Once the weather gets nice, absolutely nothing can keep me indoors."

Old habits die hard, however. A new plant still talks its way into the garden as fast as she feasts her eyes on it. Where to plant it is a worry for another day. "There's always a place if you love it," she says. ◊

Rich green foliage from trees and wildflowers serves as a foil for blue fescue (far left, foreground), golden Hinoki false cypress (left foreground), the chartreuse blooms of lady's-mantle (center foreground), blue spruce (background), and the pinks and reds of azaleas (center).

Basil Basics

Anyone can grow basil. Everyone should. It is the essence of summertime—for culinary pleasures and sure-win gardening. Whether started from seed or transplant, basil is a warm-weather friend. Plant this annual herb outdoors when the evening temperatures stay above 60 degrees. Seeds should be started indoors several weeks before the last frost date so they'll be ready to transplant outdoors when the air and soil warm.

It's easy to start basil from seed. Use 4-inch pots or 8-ounce containers (sour cream containers work well) with holes punched in the bottom. Fill the containers with damp potting soil. For best results, use a potting soil specifically made for starting seed. Put five or six seeds on top of the soil, and cover with a light layer of potting mix. Cover with plastic wrap, and keep in a warm place until the seeds germinate. Do not place in direct sun or new seedlings will scorch. Once the seeds have sprouted, remove the plastic wrap. Keep the soil moist, and move the pots into a warm, sunny spot.

The seedlings grow rapidly, filling the small pots with roots. When roots appear in the drainage holes, it's time to separate the seedlings. Tip the pots of young plants, and gently tap until they slide out. Hold the root mass in the palm of your hand, and carefully work the roots apart. Use the same potting mix to plant each basil seedling in its own container. Place the plants in a sunny window, and keep the soil slightly moist. When the weather becomes consistently warm, the basil will be ready to plant outdoors.

Growing basil is easy; deciding which selection to plant is the hard part. There's one to fit almost every culinary taste and every size garden. Basic sweet basil *(Ocimum basilicum)* is the best selection for just the good, familiar basil flavor. The large leaf types (Mammoth or

An assortment of basil planted among summer flowers makes a colorful and aromatic garden.

Remove flowerbuds to encourage new leaves for harvesting.

Lettuce Leaf) may be shredded or used whole as wrappers. New selections of citrus-flavored basils are also becoming available. Sweet Dani lemon basil, a 1998 All-America selections winner, produces branched growth and flowers late in summer. Lime basil is also a flavorful garden addition.

The Thai basils have a pungent flavor. Siam Queen grows vigorously and sports large leaves, purple stems, and purple flowers. As ornamental as it is flavorful, it tastes distinctly different than sweet basil.

Red Rubin is a new form of the older Opal basil. Used in dressings, vinegars, and jellies, its large purple leaves impart true basil flavor and jewellike color.

For growing basil in containers, several selections offer great flavor and compact size. Verde Fino looks like a small leafy shrub, growing in a small ball. It also makes a lovely annual hedge around a formal herb garden. Greek Columnar basil is a tall, narrow selection that produces tiny leaves. Although tall, it stays upright without staking and is slow to flower.

Begin with the basics. Then add at least one other selection. Summer's too short to do without.

Ellen Riley
(For sources see pages 250–251.)

Fringe Benefits Just in Time

Small trees bring a spectacular tier of flowers to the garden. Cherries and dogwoods proclaim the arrival of spring. But after all the petals have fallen, there's a lull in the garden. That's when Chinese fringe tree shows its stuff.

A relative of the spectacular native fringe tree, Chinese fringe tree *(Chionanthus retusus)* is a favorite of landscape architect Ben Page in Nashville. "It is truly one of the great plants," says Ben.

Flowering begins in late April to May, depending on where you live, and can continue into June. Rounded green leaves are festooned with clusters of white-petaled flowers that are airy and light, like fringe.

After the flowers have faded, it remains handsome in its green summer cloak. The leaves turn yellow in autumn, and then drop to reveal its second best attribute after the flowers—its trunk. "The winter interest is wonderful," says Ben, "because of the way the winter sun strikes the leathery, sinewy bark."

Although Chinese fringe tree may appear as a shrub at the nursery, it makes a fine, multitrunked tree with a little help. Removing the lower branches as it grows taller gives the plant a treelike form. Ben recommends raising the canopy about 6 to 8 inches each year.

It will grow to 15 feet or more at maturity, producing a bountiful display of flowers in late spring, as if to answer as gardeners ask, "Is that all there is?" *Linda C. Askey*

(For sources see pages 250–251.)

Chinese fringe tree offers its flowers just as much of the garden has begun to turn green.

CHINESE FRINGE TREE
At a Glance

Light: sun
Size: 15 to 25 feet
Range: Upper, Middle, and Lower South
Pests: none serious
Expect to pay: $10 to $21

PHOTOGRAPHS: SYLVIA MARTIN / LANDSCAPE ARCHITECT: BEN PAGE, NASHVILLE

A two-story home provides the perfect background for a magnificent stand of traveler's trees. The house also helps shield plants from leaf-shredding winds.

To expose the pretty crisscrossed trunk, remove lower leaves by cutting them at the base. Cut, don't tear, leaves and remove only a few layers of foliage at a time.

So look for a high wall to serve as a background for this stunning plant. "Traveler's tree is very architectural due to its form," explains Miami landscape architect Deena Bell. "The fan is very stiff; it needs a backdrop. It's best placed against a blank wall of a two-story house. Planted in the correct spot, it is unbelievable." *Jo Kellum*

Tremendous Tree

When a single leaf can grow 9 feet long, you know you're dealing with a big plant. Traveler's tree *(Ravenala madagascariensis)* often grows to 40 feet in height, so you can't just plop it anywhere in your garden. Older plants grow sturdy trunks that hold foliage aloft like giant fans. Even in immaturity, traveler's tree needs enough space to display its spectacular clumps of leaves effectively.

It's easy enough to grow this plant; heat and humidity are the main requirements. Rich, moist soil and full sun are best, but traveler's tree will tolerate poor, dry soil and partial shade. Frost is a lethal enemy, however.

Where you grow one is a much trickier topic. Though sometimes referred to as a palm, traveler's tree is more closely related to the banana and bird-of-paradise. Its coarse texture and surprising size make it a bold addition to any landscape; such drama must be handled carefully. Planted beside a single-story house, traveler's tree will dwarf the building. Planted in an open lawn, this tree will become the white elephant of the yard.

TRAVELER'S TREE
At a Glance

Size: 25 to 40 feet
Light: full sun to partial shade
Soil: rich and moist; will tolerate dry
Fertilizer: Apply gardenia/ixora food twice a year.
Range: South Florida
Comments: Forms large clumps. Single trunk with age. Given enough sunlight, traveler's tree makes an excellent large houseplant.
Expect to pay: $15 to $20 for a 3- to 4-foot-tall plant

This Rose Is for Real

If you like roses but don't like to spray and prune, this might be the rose for you. Pink Flower Carpet rose hit the market in August of 1995. This plant was showing up everywhere, always displayed in a pink plastic pot. Retail nurseries were promoting it as the ultimate ground cover. Words such as "carefree" and "disease resistant" were being thrown around. All the hype scared me away.

Seeing that it was here to stay, I decided to give this so-called bulletproof rose a try. After a couple of growing seasons, I found the plant to be very hardy. The foliage is attractive with shiny green leaves. I even planted some in a roof garden where they were watered occasionally overhead but otherwise left to fend for themselves. They just kept mounding and blooming.

During wet, rainy summers I did find black spot on some leaves on the lower limbs, but it never covered the plant or caused it to decline or defoliate. In spring and early summer, a profusion of buds and pink layered petals cover the stems. The flowers have yellow stamens and a faint, sweet fragrance.

Mark Krause, area landscaping manager at Disney's Grand Floridian Resort & Spa near Orlando, says these roses bloom nine months out of the year in their landscape. The blooms are self-cleaning, meaning they shed nicely, not hanging on to the plant and becoming an eyesore.

The Flower Carpet rose is not a carpet. It's more of a mounding shrub, growing around 30 inches tall and about 3 feet wide. Plants can be massed on a sunny slope or used to form a low, impenetrable hedge. To make a hedge, space plants 32 inches apart. They make nice additions to a flower border of mixed annuals and perennials. They even perform well in large containers, but watch where you put them because they are quite thorny.

White Flower Carpet has now been introduced, and my curiosity once again got the best of me. I planted one last spring, but the verdict is still out on this white selection. It isn't supposed to be quite as disease resistant as the pink Flower Carpet, because white roses traditionally don't have quite the vigor of pink ones. Lucinda Mays, curator of the Victory Garden at Callaway Gardens in Pine Mountain, Georgia, says, "Don't judge a rose until its third year, so time will tell how this one will perform."

If you like roses but don't like all the fuss, try pink Flower Carpet rose. And if you like to experiment and be on the cutting edge, try the white selection or the pale pink Appleblossom that's new this spring. They might be just what your garden needs. And remember, you don't have to own a sprayer and clippers to try them.

Charlie Thigpen
(For sources see pages 250–251.)

Pink Flower Carpet rose has waxy green foliage topped with a profusion of pink blooms. This plant isn't limited to the rose garden. Its minimal maintenance makes it extremely versatile.

PHOTOGRAPH: VAN CHAPLIN

No Trouble and Double

Last summer I thought maybe it was time to see the doctor. First I began to see roses growing in the shade. Then I began seeing double. After rubbing my eyes and getting a closer look, I realized I was looking at some of the new double and semidouble selections of impatiens. The flowers on these mounding plants look like tiny rose blooms.

Impatiens have always been the most popular shade annual for Southern gardens. The good news is that the new doubles and semidoubles are as simple to grow as the single selections. They're excellent for the novice gardener because once planted, occasional waterings are all it takes to keep these plants perky throughout the hot summer. The plants tell you when they need a drink. When their foliage begins to droop, it's time to water. Just a sprinkle of slow-release 12-6-6 fertilizer will give your plants a little boost.

The double and semidoubles aren't new to nurseries. They've been around for years, but some of the older selections were susceptible to tomato spotted wilt virus and performed poorly in the landscape. This scared a few growers away. Today's selections are just as tough as the singles and have been bred to grow stronger stems, which help support the heavy and numerous clusters of blooms.

We tried a few of the new Fiesta Series double impatiens to see how they would perform in our gardens and containers. The Fiesta Series comes in nine colors ranging from white to pink to red and orange. We planted the White, Pink Ruffles, Lavender Orchid, and Burgundy Rose. They mounded well and didn't get rangy looking. In fact, they were left in the ground through the fall and performed well until the first hard frost in late October.

A new semidouble selection of impatiens named Victorian Rose also worked well in the garden. This All-America selection winner has fewer petals than the doubles, but it still puts on a multipetaled show. Fluorescent pink flowers top the deep green foliage on these hardy plants. If you need a brilliant pink flower to brighten your shade garden, the Victorian Rose is for you.

If you're tired of planting the same old single impatiens, try some of the new double and semidoubles. They'll give you twice the show, and they're simple to grow. *Charlie Thigpen*

PHOTOGRAPHS: VAN CHAPLIN

(Above) *Burgundy Rose, a double impatiens from the Fiesta Series, produces colorful rosettes from summer into fall.*

(Left) *Victorian Rose, with its semidouble pink flowers, towers over the single white impatiens.*

This rectangular pond forms a cool centerpiece to a lush perennial garden. Edged with cinder blocks set over a plastic liner, it's inexpensive and easy to make.

No-Fuss Water Garden

You'd be hard-pressed to come up with a more attractive feature, dollar for dollar, than adding a garden pond. Especially one as appealing as the one pictured here. The materials list is short: cinder blocks, mortar, sand, plastic pond liner, and tubing. Just add water, plants, and maybe some fish to complete it.

"We had always wanted a lily pond," says landscape architect Patty Merson, who built the pond (with help from husband Bob Fugate and fellow landscape architect Hermann Weis) in the backyard of her Norcross, Georgia, home. "First, we laid out the dimensions of the pond with string, and then just started digging," she says. The pond is 2 feet deep, 4 feet wide, and 8 feet long.

After excavation, a 1- to 2-inch layer of sand was poured into the bottom of the pond to cushion the liner. Then ½-inch-diameter copper tubing was laid around the top edge. The tubing serves as a solid, level frame for the blocks as well as a smooth edge for the liner. Next came the plastic liner, which was rolled on top of the tubing. Three (¼-inch) plastic tubes laid on top of the liner at ground level serve as overflow drains.

The row of cinder blocks around the pond was then mortared in place; additional rows of blocks were laid in sand to form a small terrace around the pond.

After the mortar had set, the pond was filled, allowed to sit overnight, and then a few goldfish were added. More goldfish and plants—water lilies and yellow flag iris—were added later.

Patty decided against including any filters or pumps to keep the water clean. "Over time, the pond establishes and maintains its own balance," she says. "This is a function of water depth, plant, and fish combinations."

You might think that a pond such as this would be swarming with mosquitoes—not so. "The fish and the frogs eat the eggs," Patty says. And because there are no pumps or filters, upkeep is a breeze. "It stays clear nearly year-round, and we clean it every few years.

"We've had this pond for about 12 years," says Patty. "It's brought a wonderful dimension to the garden. The frogs, dragonflies, fish, and other wildlife are interesting to watch. We like to turn the lights on at night and count the frogs convening on the edge of the pond. Their voices are wonderful!"

Mark G. Stith

cinder block, 4 x 8 x 16 solid core

cinder block, 4 x 8 x 16 hollow core

3 (¼-inch) drain tubes

1- to 2-inch overhang

sand

½-inch copper tubing

2'

4'

mortar

clay soil

pond liner

1 to 2 inches of sand

Backstage at the Garden

Behind the scenes of Tom and Joan MacCubbin's Orlando garden lies a work area that is organized but comfortable, logical but fun. One look at the MacCubbin's potting bench tells you these folks are serious about gardening. Tom is the urban horticulturist for Orange County and shares his expertise in gardening through radio, television, books, and newspapers. Joan is with him step for step. We asked Tom about his work area, how he set it up, and what he feels is essential.

Think big. "Make it large enough so you have room to spread out, and have pots handy," Tom recommends. "Plenty of room is the key to success."

Buy trash cans. "We put our soil components in trash cans—vermiculite in one, perlite in another, compost or lime in another," says Tom. "And there are scoops inside each one." His storage system keeps materials dry and clean.

Buy more trash cans. "We store our soil mix in another trash can," says Tom. "Trash cans keep all these things accessible for us. My wife is always asking me to mix up more soil. I mix it up in a small trash can that I tumble manually." Tom also keeps a trash can with a solution of 1 part chlorine bleach to 10 parts water for sterilizing pots he plans to reuse.

Underfoot. Tom has concrete paved surfaces where work can get messy or where he needs a firm surface to roll a garden cart. "We just hose it down," he says.

Have a sink. "It is so handy having a sink outside," Tom observes. "You can wash pots in it; you can wash hands. We have soap right there, and I normally attach a towel to my belt." He recommends having a cutoff valve in areas where the pipes might freeze. They would be less likely to freeze if the sink is located next to the house.

Lots of pots. "We keep only the standard sizes—3, 4, and 6 inches, and maybe some larger ones," says Tom. "And we keep only the ones we use. You can get odd sizes, and it's hard to stack them."

Built to last. Tom's workbench is constructed of pressure-treated pine. "We wouldn't have anything else in Florida," he says. *Linda C. Askey*

Tom and Joan keep only the pots they really use. They're washed, stacked, and ready when needed. Sterilizing the pots with a mixture of chlorine bleach and water kills any soilborne diseases that may be present.

PHOTOGRAPHS: VAN CHAPLIN

The MacCubbin's potting area is well organized but obviously used. Anything Tom or Joan needs is at their fingertips.

How do you get different looks from ordinary pots? It's simple; you stack them. Last spring I went to a garden center and purchased terra-cotta pots of all shapes and sizes. The pots were inexpensive, and they looked great once they were filled with soil, stacked, and planted. Annuals, herbs, and plants with attractive foliage fill these piggyback pots.

I used bagged topsoil instead of potting soil to fill the containers. Potting soil tends to be spongy and won't pack firmly. Topsoil provides a stable base for the pots. In some of the large containers, two bricks set inside create a level surface. The deeper you sink the upper pot into the lower pot the greater the stability.

Make sure that your containers are secure by using both hands to work the upper pot into the lower one. Then fill around the upper pot with soil, and pack it firmly. When filled, the pots will be heavy. Make sure that they are stable and not located in high traffic areas or close to children's play areas.

For the arrangement shown at left, I placed a small strawberry jar in the center of a large bowl-shaped container, topped the jar with asparagus fern, and filled the side holes with petunias. Then I planted dwarf mondo grass and creeping Jenny in the bowl-shaped container.

piggyback pots

For the planting shown at far right, I placed a large 5-gallon strawberry jar in a bigger container and filled them with herbs such as rosemary, thyme, parsley, and oregano. (Herbs and other plants that require well-drained soil perform wonderfully in strawberry jars.) The pots filled out nicely, and the plants were a tasty addition to the garden. Even in the winter months, I was able to harvest from this miniature herb garden.

The three-tiered planter (shown at right) was created with different-size rolled-rim containers. Pink petunias spill over the edge of the base pot. Begonias and asparagus fern fill the middle, while Mexican heather and a Blue Pyramid cypress point skyward in the top pot.

The shade-lovers combination (shown at left) created a neat display. Creeping fig and dwarf mondo grass fill the base container, and three upside-down orchid pots form feet to support a pot of strawberry geraniums and Japanese painted fern.

Potting all these combinations took less than a half-day. Because containers come in so many shapes and sizes, it's like putting a puzzle together. It's fun to stack a few and see if the pieces fit. ◇

Three upside-down orchid pots elevate a container of strawberry geraniums and Japanese painted fern.

BY CHARLIE THIGPEN
PHOTOGRAPHY JEAN ALLSOPP

(Far left) *Stacked terra-cotta pots create a minigarden.*

(Left) *This three-tiered planting is tall and colorful. Each level has a totally different look.*

(Below) *These two pots filled with herbs are a tasty treat.*

Two bricks placed side by side in this container will provide a stable base for another pot.

Jacob and the Bean Stalk

BY CHARLIE THIGPEN
PHOTOGRAPHY VAN CHAPLIN

Brian Bender (right) and Jacob pick beans and play in and around the bean house. The tiny house acts as a trellis for pole beans planted around its perimeter.

Any father would be proud to build and give his son a new house. Needless to say, I was excited the first day I took my son, Jacob, to see the house I was constructing for him. We walked up to it and I waited for a response. Jacob studied the house then said, "Daddy, there's no door." A father's work is never done.

It was back to the woods in search of a few thick, supple vines. I bent the vines and added a few sticks to form an arching door. I think he liked the door because he could keep me out. I didn't really care. I was just glad that he was outside playing and not glued to the television set. Little did he know that this structure would soon have pole beans to form walls and a roof.

Jacob's stick house was framed up with the limbs and the trunks of two mimosa trees. The largest pieces of wood from the trunks of the trees form the four corner posts of the house. I used posthole diggers to dig four holes, and set each post about 2 feet in the ground. Then I filled around the posts, tamping the soil until each one was sturdy and secure.

Now it was time to use a little imagination to attach the sides and the roof. I didn't use a level, hammer, or nails. A small pruning saw and clippers were the only tools needed. Wire and string held everything together. I left Y-shaped crotches on some of the limbs so they could be used to support crossing limbs. A gridlike pattern of limbs made the roof look like square shingles and provided a nice support for the vining beans. I wove some of the horizontal branches through the vertical ones to make the roof tight and sturdy.

Once the house was complete, some landscaping was needed. I tilled the soil around the house and used a hard rake to break up the dirt clods and remove any rocks. When the soil was loose, I planted a few perennials and scattered zinnia and cosmos seeds for quick and inex-

pensive color. Painted gourds, hung along the roofline, add the finishing touch.

I planted a single row of Kentucky Wonder pole bean seeds at a depth of 1 to 1½ inches and about 4 to 6 inches apart on the sides and back of the house. I watered them every couple of days and, once the plants emerged and were 3 to 4 inches tall, I side-dressed them with a little slow-release vegetable fertilizer.

The vines grew quickly, covering the house. The beans produced by the bucket load, and Jacob and I picked them

A small window box shaped from chicken wire and lined with burlap makes an inexpensive planter.

together. We ate the beans two or three times a week and still gave plenty away.

Houses are supposed to be an excellent investment, and that's true of Jacob's bean house. Any brush that you clear or small tree that you cut can be used to construct a little house. Lumber won't cost you a dime. A few rolls of rope might cost $5 or $6, and a couple of packs of bean seeds will cost around $3.

This investment really paid off for me. My family received plenty of meals from the beans, Jacob had a place that he could call his own, and he also learned a little about gardening. Now he knows that green beans don't just come from a can or the supermarket. ◇

THE INTREPID GARDENER

At first, all Ram Giberson could grow was patience. When she finally started her garden after more than a decade of dreaming, she dug in with fearless determination.

BY JO KELLUM
PHOTOGRAPHY JEAN ALLSOPP

A garden filled with sunflowers, zinnias, melampodium, red coleus, and other summer plants (See pages 134–136.)

June

Checklist
for
June

EDITORS' NOTEBOOK

In gardening, we often discover a wealth of "truths" that are logical, self-evident, and absolutely wrong. Blueberries are a good example. When are they ready to pick? When they first turn blue? It's logical. It's reasonable. It's also wrong. They generally reach their peak of sweetness four to seven days after they turn completely blue. Make them even sweeter by treating them to some extra potassium. Sprinkle a cupful of potassium sulfate (not muriate of potash, which can burn roots) around each bush in fall. You can order it from Peaceful Valley Farm Supply at (916) 272-4769. Of course, not every logical-sounding assumption is erroneous. For instance, what's a foolproof sign blueberries are at their peak? That's right—when you discover a cloud of birds stripping off every berry. *Steve Bender*

□ **Daylilies**—To decide the best colors and heights for your garden, select daylilies while they are in bloom. Dwarf types may be used for borders while larger ones are best suited as middle and background perennials. Mass landscape types to form a ground cover for sunny areas. Some that bloom several times during the summer include Yellow Bouquet, Bitsy, Pink Flirt, Cajun Gambler, and Scarlet Orbit.

□ **Hibiscus**—Root your favorite hibiscus by taking 6-inch cuttings from the tips of stems and dipping the cut ends in rooting hormone. Stick them in pots of sterile seed-starter mix. Cover each new plant with an inverted glass jar to keep it moist. Place in indirect light, and water regularly. In six weeks, you can uncover the rooted cuttings and let them grow. ▶

□ **Houseplants**—Plants that have become too large for their pots or have declined from soil compaction will benefit from new pots and fresh soil. Slip the roots out of the old pot, shake off a portion of the old soil by tapping the root ball on a hard surface; then repot in a container that is larger than the original pot by at least 2 inches in diameter.

Move plants outside to cool, shaded garden beds for the summer. Sink the pots halfway into the ground to keep them from turning over and to conserve moisture.

□ **Southern magnolia**—Don't be alarmed by magnolias that have been dropping their leaves. It's normal for this evergreen to shed some of its older foliage now.

□ **Sprinklers**—If the spray from your sprinkler is blocked by tall plants, elevate it. Place the sprinkler on a bucket or similar support. Put a brick on the base of the sprinkler to stabilize it.

□ **Squash**—If your flowers are falling off without growing any squash, they may be male flowers. Female flowers have a tiny squash below the flower; male flowers have only a stem. Many times the first flowers are male; the female ones will develop in a few days.

□ **Vegetables**—Harvest beans, cucumbers, okra, and squash daily. They pass their tender stage quickly. Harvest eggplant while small and glossy; mature fruit forms bitter seeds inside.

□ **Vines**—Train the new growth of clematis, yellow jessamine, and other twining vines to guide them onto the trellis. The new canes of climbing roses usually need some help too. Use loose, dark green twist ties to hold the new growth in place.

□ **Water**—When the first hot days arrive, remember all the new trees, shrubs, and perennials you planted this spring. Check them for signs of drought. Water deeply at least once each rainless week.

□ **Annuals**—Plant heat-tolerant annuals, such as globe amaranth, cockscomb, cleome, cosmos, zinnia, portulaca, periwinkle, sunflowers, and tithonia, from seed or transplants.

□ **Bulbs**—Dividing clumps every three to five years encourages more flowers and provides you with more bulbs. As soon as their foliage turns yellow, spring bulbs such as narcissus and leucojum (snowflakes) may be dug and divided. Using a spading fork, loosen and lift entire clumps, and carefully remove the soil from the roots and bulbs. Separate individual bulbs, and replant immediately; or store the bulbs in a shady, well-ventilated area until September or October.

□ **Caladiums**—Even medium-size tubers (about 2 inches in diameter) can provide quick displays in shaded beds. Space 12 to 15 inches apart in well-prepared soil. Water every three to four days during dry periods. ▶

□ **Iris**—Bearded types can be transplanted while in bloom. Actually, that is the best time to buy because you can see the color. You can also divide and replant existing clumps after they bloom.

□ **Jacaranda**—In South Texas and South Florida, plant shade-tolerant agapanthus under a jacaranda tree for a stunning combination. Both bloom now, in shades of blue.

□ **Palm trees**—Palms fare best when planted during the rainy season in Florida. Get new ones in the ground this month or next. Add a palm fertilizer that contains iron, manganese, and magnesium, elements often lacking in sandy soil.

□ **Perennials**—Plant fall-blooming perennials, such as Mexican bush sage *(Salvia leucantha),* Mexican mint marigold *(Tagetes lucida),* white rain lilies *(Zephyranthes candida),* and garden mums now for blooms beginning in September.

PRUNE

□ **Chrysanthemums**—Keep mums from getting too tall by cutting back to about half their height. Continue pinching new growth through June to encourage branching.

CONTROL

□ **Grubs**—The larvae of June beetles and Japanese beetles will damage roots of turf, as well as other plants. You can apply carbaryl to kill adults, but you'll have to reapply after every rain. Milky spore powder is a biological control that kills grubs in the soil for up to 20 years without harming people or pets.

FERTILIZE

□ **Amaryllis**—Feed amaryllis with a slow-release fertilizer such as 9-9-6. In summer, the bulbs store energy and develop next year's blooms.

□ **Azaleas and camellias**—These shrubs develop next year's blooms now, so be sure to water if they go without rain. Renew mulch over their roots. Fertilize with an azalea-camellia food that contains iron and other micronutrients.

□ **Flowers**—Annual and perennial beds can use a boost, especially where the soil is sandy or the season has been rainy. Apply slow-release fertilizer for maximum benefit with minimum effort. For a quick but brief effect, water plants with soluble 20-20-20.

□ **Lawns**—Apply 16-4-8 or similar fertilizer to all warm-season lawns except centipede. Be sure to buy a product that includes at least 30% slow-release nitrogen to feed your lawn evenly and to reduce the nutrients that wash away. Use the rate recommended on the label.

□ **Roses**—In addition to regular feedings, boost your roses weekly during the rainy season with an extra dose of soluble fertilizer such as 20-20-20.

June notes:

TIP OF THE MONTH

We used to grow our pole beans on a traditional bamboo tepee, with the poles tied together at the top. But the beans were hard to pick. Now we slant our bamboo poles outward instead of inward. This provides more light and air for the plants. It also makes picking easy, because the beans hang freely.

TOBY AND REESE DANLEY KILGO
HUNTSVILLE, ALABAMA

FLEA MARKET
fountains

BY CHARLIE THIGPEN
PHOTOGRAPHY VAN CHAPLIN

Ordinary objects make a splash in the garden, proving that one man's trash may be a water gardener's treasure.

As cicadas scream about the heat on a sultry afternoon, the splash of water can cool down summer's sizzle. And—good news—fountains aren't limited to upscale neighborhoods or fancy public gardens.

We came up with a few unusual water features made from salvaged finds ranging from an old musical instrument to broken pottery. These eye- *and* ear-catching fountains are inexpensive and easy to make.

We purchased pumps, plants, and pond liners from a local garden center and bought plumbing parts and silicone at a hardware store.

We made the fountain shown at right from a brass horn we found at a flea market. It was banged up and tarnished just enough to give it character. A simple metal stand keeps the instrument upright. We punched a small hole in the bottom of the horn so a piece of copper tubing could be inserted. Next we attached a pump to one end of the tubing

(Left) *Blast from the past. An old horn sat idle for years. Now it plays a sweet melody in the garden.* **(Far left)** *Nestled among plants, this rustic urn pours water into the pool.* **(Above)** *When you don't have a lot of room for a water feature, this self-contained fountain is a portable option. It recirculates water from the spigot to the pail.*

and a flower-spray fountain head to the other end. The wide spraying pattern of the fountain head simulates music coming from the horn.

If you use a wide spray head, make sure that the spray pattern is half the size of the pool so water won't splash outside the perimeter. This pool is circular in shape and about 12 feet across—the spray pattern is about 6 feet across. The horn made such a big show that it needed a large space to be in scale.

The fountain shown at far left rests on the edge of a small 3-foot-wide pool. We spotted and rescued an urn with broken handles in a garbage pile. Peeling white paint reveals its natural color.

There was already a drainage hole in the bottom of the urn, so it was easy to run a piece of plastic tubing from the pump into the container. The urn tilts just enough to allow the water to spill into the pool with a soothing splash. The new pool takes on an aged look with the addition of the crumbling urn.

A small fountain made from a watering pail takes up little space and creates a nice sound.

We punched two holes in the back side of the pail. The pump cord fits through the upper hole. The lower hole accommodates a pipe so that water can be recirculated.

The fountain shown above doesn't need a pool to sit in. The simple self-contained unit takes up little room. It can be used on a deck or any small nook in the garden. A faucet pours continuously into the pail, creating a nice ringing tone.

This fountain took some rigging and a little explaining at the hardware store. We attached galvanized pipe to the side of the pail with a coupling and sealed it with silicone. Plastic tubing runs through the pipe and faucet. The pump connected to the tubing recirculates the water.

These three fountains are all different, yet each one enhances the garden. Pumps were the most expensive element of the water features. The large fountain with the horn uses a pump that moves 500 gallons of water per hour and cost approximately $120. The urn fountain uses a medium-size pump that runs 300 gallons per hour and cost approximately $70. The watering pail fountain uses a small pump rated at 90 gallons per hour and cost around $60.

Pumps can be expensive, so take care of them. Keep your fountain and pump intake clean. Never tug or lift the pump by its cord—it can cause electrical leakage and damage your pump. Make sure to plug your pump into a ground fault outlet only.

While the sweltering heat of summer bears down on the garden, add a water feature. Water is the essential element of life; pump a little life into your garden. ◇

Annabelle hydrangea produces a spectacular display of enormous white flowers that last and last.

Annabelle Shines in Summer Shade

From boring to beautiful in three easy steps. That may sound like an ad for a charm school, but it's also a good description of how to make a shady corner of your yard sparkle. Step 1: Buy a 1- to 3-gallon container of Annabelle hydrangea. Step 2: Plant it, and water regularly. Step 3: Stand back, and be prepared to accept compliments.

This hydrangea (*Hydrangea arborescens* Annabelle) isn't the shy, retiring type that blends into the background. Standing alone or as part of a border, it is a show-off that's sensational in woodland gardens.

It would be difficult not to notice dense, globular flower clusters up to a foot across, especially when they almost cover a shrub that quickly grows 3 to 5 feet tall and about 5 feet wide. Unlike many flowers that rapidly fade away in the South's heat and humidity, Annabelle's pristine white blooms lend a feeling of coolness to the landscape for at least a month.

Annabelle will feel right at home when planted in rich, well-drained,

ANNABELLE HYDRANGEA
At a Glance

Light: partial shade to shade
Soil: rich, moist, well drained
Moisture: ample water during dry spells
Pests: few
Propagation: cuttings in July; division of clumps
Range: throughout the South
Expect to pay: $15 to $25

moist soil. It isn't the least bit fussy about pH, so it will be happy whether your soil is acid or alkaline.

In a border, good neighbors for Annabelle hydrangea are impatiens, White Nancy lamium, Francee hosta, or a variegated carex such as *C. conica* Marginata. If you've chosen a spot with a half-day's sun, consider daylilies as sidekicks because many of them bloom at the same time as Annabelle. A lightly shaded walkway will make quite an impression with massed red or pink daylilies lining one side and Annabelle on the other.

Care is simple: regular watering during dry spells and once-a-year pruning. To get the biggest blooms and more of them, cut Annabelle back to within a foot of the ground in late winter because flowers are produced on new wood. This also helps keep the shrub compact.

The choice is yours. Settle for a sea of green in partial shade, or let Annabelle light up the dark corners in spectacular fashion. *Judy Lowe*

(For sources see pages 250–251.)

Celosia Worth a Second Look

If you think celosia is just a squatty little annual best used for filling flowerbeds with flamelike blooms of red, orange, and gold, it's time to take a second look. Meet the wheat celosias *(Celosia spicata)*, which grow 3 to 4 feet tall and hold bright-tipped flowers aloft on slender stalks.

Two selections of wheat celosia commonly available are aptly named. Pink Candle glows with hundreds of blossoms from summer into fall. Pink, wheatlike blooms start off small and elongate with age. By late summer, the pale flowers are cylindrical, tapering into bright pink points. Purple Flamingo sports leggy, purplish stems bearing dark blossoms spiked with almost fluorescent tips. This selection grows slightly taller than Pink Candle, so be sure to plant Purple Flamingo in the back of the bed if you're mixing the two.

Both selections make lovely cut flowers for fresh or dried arrangements. To dry, clip blossoms and hang them upside down in a warm, dry

place for a week or more. Flowers will retain their color for about a year before fading.

If you don't have wheat celosia growing in your garden this year, order seeds to sow next spring shortly after the last frost. Seedlings may need some protection against marauding slugs, but mature plants are normally pest free and drought tolerant. Both Pink Candle and Purple Flamingo prefer full sun and well-drained soil. Deadhead your plants occasionally for continuous flowering throughout the hot months.

Unlike many summer flowers, which appear tired and ragged by season's end, wheat celosia stays lovely until freezing temperatures arrive. Though the foliage may droop, flowers drying on their stalks can withstand light frost. This makes wheat celosia an excellent choice to help tide the garden through that transitional time between sunflowers and mums. *Jo Kellum*

(For sources see pages 250–251.)

PHOTOGRAPHS: TINA CORNETT / LOCATION: THE BILTMORE ESTATE, ASHEVILLE, NORTH CAROLINA

WHEAT CELOSIA
At a Glance

Size: 3 to 4 feet high
Light: full sun
Soil: well drained
Range: all South
Note: You'll have volunteer seedlings for seasons to come.
Expect to pay: about $2 per seed packet

Pink Candle and Purple Flamingo wheat celosia make a striking pair against a background of cosmos.

PHOTOGRAPH: TINA CORNETT / OWNER: LIZ TEDDER, NEWNAN, GEORGIA

Glory for the Summer

When our annual summer heat wave begins, think of your garden as a little slice of Florida. You may not have a beach in your backyard, but you can grow some bright-blooming tropical plants that usually prosper only in the Sunshine State.

Glory bush is one worth trying. A loose, gangly shrub with fuzzy leaves, glory bush is known for its velvety purple flowers. Blooms occur on the tips of branches, with a scattered show of color appearing nonstop until frost. Plant it in the back of a sunny border where it can provide a background to shorter flowers. Or try it in a container for a summer surprise.

This plant likes sun—the hotter, the better. Though it doesn't require excessive amounts of water, rain is plentiful in tropical regions in the summer, so glory bush does need a good drenching every now and then. Plants growing in pots require more water than those growing in the ground.

If you want to overwinter your plant, grow it on the south side of your home in a protected location, mulch well, and pray. The Brazilian form of glory bush

GLORY BUSH
At a Glance

Size: 4 to 6 feet tall in a summer
Light: full sun
Soil: fertile, well drained, slightly acid
Range: permanent in Central and Southern Florida; may be considered seasonal color throughout the South
Expect to pay: $6 for a 1-gallon plant; $14 to $16 for a 3-gallon Athens Blue; $16 to $20 for a standard-form Athens Blue

(Tibouchina urvilleana) may be the best bet for withstanding brief cold snaps and reappearing again in the spring. If you're really dedicated, pot up plants and bring them indoors for the winter. But unless you live where temperatures rarely dip into the 20s and the ground doesn't freeze, you're probably better off considering glory bush as a big annual worth replacing each year. Though new plants are costly, the size and impression glory bush contributes to your garden make it a good value when compared with smaller annuals. And you'll enjoy it for six months or more.

Another form of this tropical plant, *T. semidecandra grandiflora,* originated in New Zealand; a large-blooming form was introduced by The University of Georgia. Named Athens Blue, this selection of glory bush puts on a bigger show of flowers. It's a great choice for a colorful summer guest in your garden. If you're lucky, you may find Athens Blue grown as a standard, shaped like a miniature tree with a single trunk crowned with flowers and foliage. Needless to say, it is glorious.

Jo Kellum

Yellow shrimp plant is easy to grow and supplies bright color in the garden from spring until frost. Red lantana makes a good companion.

A Smashing Success

One of the great things about gardening is that every year you have the chance to try something new. Granted, some experiments don't pan out. But others succeed magnificently, and you're richer for it.

A recent personal triumph involved a plant unfamiliar to most folks—yellow shrimp plant *(Pachystachys lutea)*. It's semitropical, meaning that it's perennial in the Coastal and Tropical South, but elsewhere you treat it as an annual. I wanted something different and eye-catching to supply color in front of my house throughout the summer. Boy, did I make the right choice.

Like many tropical and semitropical plants, yellow shrimp plant blooms continuously in warm weather. In my garden, that means May through October. The bloom you notice from a distance is not a true flower, but a cone of overlapping yellow bracts. The true flowers are white and creep out of the bracts like ghosts emerging in the night. Even though the blooms aren't red, hummingbirds like them just the same.

Caring for yellow shrimp plant is simple. You don't have to remove spent flowers because they drop off automatically to make way for new ones. All the plant basically wants is full sun and well-drained soil. To get a bushier plant and more blooms, cut back the main stems by several inches after planting. Always cut back to a node (the point where leaves sprout from the stem). Each cut stem will produce two new stems. Feed it every two to three weeks with a high-phosphorus, bloom-booster fertilizer.

Look for yellow shrimp plant at local garden centers, home-center stores, and greenhouses. You'll probably see it recommended as an indoor plant only. Don't believe it. A plant this showy needs to be seen out front. *Steve Bender*

YELLOW SHRIMP PLANT
At a Glance

Light: full sun
Soil: moist, well drained, fertile
Size: to 3 feet tall and wide in most locations
Pests: occasional scales, mealybugs, spider mites
Prune: early spring
Range: winter-hardy only in Coastal and Tropical South
Expect to pay: $5 to $10 for large plants

Everything's All White

Fay Ireland's garden in Shoal Creek, Alabama, is filled with plants of all sizes, shapes, and colors, but outside her kitchen window they're all white.

Why white? Dark flowers and foliage tend to get lost and disappear as the sun sets, but white is visible even under low-light conditions. Flowers twinkling at dusk and dawn allow more time to enjoy the garden. In the heat of summer, white always appears fresh and clean and has a cooling effect, when just *looking* at bright colors, such as red, yellow, or orange, can make you sweat.

Perennials and biennials, such as daisies, feverfew, phlox, and veronica make up the bulk of the garden. Begonias, impatiens, pansies, petunias, and other white-flowering annuals weave through the mix. They're changed seasonally to fill in holes. White Rose-of-Sharon and crepe myrtles grow tall and add needed height. Most of these plants aren't exotic or hard to find.

Those with variegated and silvery foliage also play a key role. Snow-in-summer has frosted foliage, and its small leaves add a lacy texture. White-and-green variegated Algerian ivy creeps up the walls, creating a lush backdrop. When blooms are few, foliage holds the garden together.

"If it's white, it's been in there," says Mrs. Ireland of the many plants she has tried and tested. This, like every garden, is for learning. Each year is different, and every season brings change.

Charlie Thigpen

White Swirl Siberian iris

Sister Theresa hydrangea fills this shady corner, while begonias and impatiens flower below.

PHOTOGRAPHS: JEAN ALLSOPP, VAN CHAPLIN

The view from Fay Ireland's kitchen window reveals clouds of white flowers and foliage that wrap the garden path.

In Touch With Lamb's-ears

Aptly named and ever welcome, the plant known as lamb's-ears is a gardener's version of a huggable stuffed toy.

One glimpse of this silvery perennial and it will capture your heart. Its leafy mat of shimmering foliage complements more colorful neighbors. But even when it grows solo, it draws admiration.

Spreading into a blanket of silver, lamb's-ears *(Stachys byzantina)* makes a showy ground cover, and it adds a spark to flowerbeds where it will fill the front edge and spill over softly like a fur collar.

The secret to success with lamb's-ears is to give it good drainage. Soggy soil is certain death. Even in raised beds, summer rains that persist for several days will make a healthy clump of it melt before your eyes. At times like these, slosh into your garden as soon as possible, and pull the mat of dead leaves from beneath the healthy ones. They will stick together like a solid layer of wool felt. Removing this will increase air circulation and hopefully stop the rot.

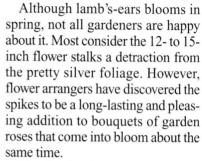

This large-leaved selection called Helen von Stein, or Big Ears, is more resistant to summer rains than the common form.

Like most silver plants, including artemisia, santolina, and snow-in-summer, lamb's-ears enjoys plenty of sun. However, gardeners in the warmer regions of the Middle South and cooler portions of the Lower South would be wise to give plants a little shade, particularly in the afternoon.

Although lamb's-ears blooms in spring, not all gardeners are happy about it. Most consider the 12- to 15-inch flower stalks a detraction from the pretty silver foliage. However, flower arrangers have discovered the spikes to be a long-lasting and pleasing addition to bouquets of garden roses that come into bloom about the same time.

If gathering lamb's-ears for cut flowers is not for you, try a selection called Silver Carpet. It is so happy growing pretty leaves that it forgets to bloom.

EDITOR'S CHOICE

Although named for a German princess, the selection called Countess Helen von Stein (or Big Ears) appears to be more tolerant of our Southern heat and humidity than others of the species. In addition, its oversize leaves are real attention-grabbers, and it is reluctant to flower, at least in my garden.

Linda C. Askey

LAMB'S-EARS
At a Glance

Personality: lovable, leafy mat of soft silvery leaves

How to grow: Plant in sun and well-drained soil.

Blooms: late April and May, not always welcome

Height: 4 to 15 inches, depending on the season

Nice to know: Pull out matted leaves after rainy spells.

Range: Upper, Middle, and cooler portions of the Lower South

Expect to pay: $5 to $8 per plant, depending on the selection

Low-growing and mat-forming, lamb's-ears is an ideal ground cover for this entry garden.

High-Value Vegetables

We've all seen them in the grocery stores, beautiful peppers in the colors of the rainbow. And you need that pot of gold at the end to pay for them. But if you dig down into your pocket for a little "seed money," your results will be less expensive, more flavorful, and more exotic. Growing your own vegetables couldn't be easier. Many garden shops are beginning to carry gourmet vegetable seedlings in ready-to-plant packs. Catalogs also offer a fascinating array of seeds. If you're short on space, many vegetables can be grown in containers. The produce is not only tasty; it's lovely as well.

Freshness and flavor are the real benefits of growing specialty vegetables. The trip from garden to table is only a few short steps.

Some high-value vegetables prefer cool weather, and others insist on warm soil. If you're growing warm-weather vegetables from seed, you can sow them directly in garden when the soil has warmed sufficiently. Or to get a get a jump on the growing season, start them indoors in early spring. Cool-weather vegetables can be seeded directly or transplanted into the garden. Know the plant's preferences, and it's hard to go wrong. *Ellen Riley*

HIGH-VALUE VEGETABLES FOR WARM WEATHER

Vegetable & Variety	Adapts to Container
Sweet Peppers	
Yellow—Lemon Belle	Y
Orange—Valencia	Y
Red—Vidi	Y
Purple—Chocolate Beauty	Y
Cream—Ivory Charm	Y
Eggplant	
White—Asian Bride	Y
Lavender—Rosa Bianca	Y
Long—Little Fingers	Y
Small—Slim Jim	Y
Tomatoes	
Yellow—Yellow Pear, Mandarin Cross	N
Pink—Brandywine	N
Striped—Big Rainbow	N
Plum—La Rossa	N
Squash	
Patty Pan—yellow Sunburst scallop	N
Zucchini—Ronde de Nice	N
Spaghetti—Hasta la Pasta	N
Lettuces	
Mesclun mixes	Y
Spring mixes	Y
Cutting mixes	Y
Master chef blend	Y

HIGH-VALUE VEGETABLES FOR COOL WEATHER

Vegetable & Variety	Adapts to Container
Edible Podded Peas	
Snow peas	N
Cascadia	N
Sugar Snap	N
Radishes	
Easter Egg Mix	Y
Flamboyant	Y
Misato Rose	Y

(For sources see pages 250–251.)

PHOTOGRAPH: VAN CHAPLIN

What was once a simple deck beside the farmhouse is now an elegant bridge between home and garden.

ALL IN LINE

BY LINDA C. ASKEY
PHOTOGRAPHY VAN CHAPLIN

When garden designer Dabney Peeples bought his Easley, South Carolina, farmhouse, the living room opened onto a simple deck on the side of the house. It had a railing around it, and there were two steps right beside the house, leading to the backyard.

"Because the deck is just 12 inches off the ground here, we just took the railing down and redirected the steps. That's one of the most common things we do in our office,"

BEFORE

Dabney says of his firm, JDP Design Associates, Inc. With assistance from business partner Art Campbell, Dabney developed a view into the garden and framed it with a pergola.

The focus of the view is a pair of Adirondack chairs and a birdhouse, set amid summer color. Using a straight line in this manner is a simple but powerful device that gives a garden structure. The line from the deck to distant chairs unites the house with the garden beyond and creates a subtle yet compelling invitation to come out and see what's blooming.

The 6 x 6 posts of the pergola are detailed with a chamfered edge and ringed with back-to-back cove molding.

One aspect that makes this garden so appealing is the scale of the pergola. "I tell my clients, 'Don't be scared of bigness outdoors,'" Dabney explains. "When I say something is going to be 10 feet tall and 13, 14, or 80 feet long, people say, 'Good heavens, we're not building the aqueduct in Rome.' But numbers diminish when you go outside."

This pergola measures 6 feet wide and 8 feet tall at the horizontal pieces. The 18-inch peak raises the height to 9½ feet. The posts are 6 x 6s; the peak is made of 4 x 4s. The two wings on either side frame the view of the garden while defining the edge of the deck.

Two oversize pots sit in a bed of creeping liriope (*Liriope spicata*) on each side of the pergola. They hold variegated Hinoki false cypress (*Chamaecyparis obtusa*), English ivy, and Purple Wave petunias. But the sight was not always so perfect. "The pots were Clemson-orange terra-cotta," says Dabney. An aged appearance was achieved with a diluted solution of dark green paint (see "Instant Age" below). "It immediately looks like old scuzz," he says with a grin.

With the design of the garden well established, there is a lot of flexibility in planting. Sun-loving color clusters around the pair of chairs, and pine straw paths mark a circular route to more shaded areas. When Dabney is given a plant, he explains, "I do what I tell clients not to do; I get a plant and then try to find a place to put it." ◇

(For sources see pages 250–251.)

Simplicity is the key. The focus of the garden lies in two white chairs and a birdhouse cloaked with summer flowers.

INSTANT AGE

To give new pots an aged look, Art used a dark green latex paint diluted with water (1 part paint to 5 parts water). First, wet either terra-cotta or concrete pots with a garden hose. Then crumple newspaper, dip it in diluted paint, and dab it on the pots.

Pots With Impact

When planting multiple pots on your porch this summer, remember repetition. Try repeating a color or plant in each pot to tie them together. Don't put 10 different colors on one porch. Too many shades or shapes will appear chaotic and cluttered.

Take a look at this planting and how all four pots work together. Five caladiums, a spider plant, and a Little Gem magnolia dress up the steps and porch. Red caladiums on the steps complement the large pot in the corner.

Low-growing plants work well on the steps, and a 5-foot-tall Little Gem magnolia fills the corner, while helping to hide a downspout. Not only are the plants cohesive, but the containers also have a similar look.

Before plant shopping make a list of what you'll need. Here are some things to consider.

■ Check to see if you have sun or shade.
■ Which size plants will you need?
■ How many plants will you need?
■ Do you want short, mounding plants or tall ones?
■ Which colors will complement your house, not clash with it?
■ How much time are you willing to spend watering?
■ Do you need potting soil?
■ Consider small trees and shrubs. They work beautifully in large containers.

Your porch doesn't have to be covered in plants to be inviting. A few pots placed and planted strategically can be visually appealing and give you more bang for your buck. *Charlie Thigpen*

The containers on this porch are simple yet bold. No flowers grace these pots, but the foliage provides plenty of impact.

OASIS IN OKLAHOMA CITY

BY STEVE BENDER
PHOTOGRAPHY ALLEN ROKACH

Here's a garden anyone would crave. And, believe it or not, it all came to be because the backyard had gone to the dog.

It seems that Hal and Marilyn Balyeat's chocolate Lab had taken command of their entire yard. But they wanted a flower garden and an orderly place to entertain. Landscape architect Warren Edwards showed them the way.

He divided the yard into two sections—a formal lawn and garden next to the house and an informal lawn in back where the dog can run. The green lattice fencing partitioning the yard has several benefits. It creates a sense of enclosure without seeming claustrophobic. It also supports roses, wisteria, clematis, and other climbers, adding extra privacy.

Finally, its open framework lets in the breeze, a vital consideration in Oklahoma City in the summertime.

Two features serve as focal points. The first, a fountain that's a family heirloom, rests in the middle of a bright green fescue lawn. The second, a custom-made arbor set on axis with the back porch, offers a welcome retreat. Arches of galvanized pipe and wire mesh atop the arbor sustain grape vines, climbing roses, and other shade providers. Warren explains that he selected the pipe because "it's extremely effective, nonintrusive, and very strong."

Curving brick walls with flagstone caps enclose the symmetrical lawn on two sides. Behind them, English-style perennial borders supply summerlong color. To help the

No, this isn't Giverny, Sissinghurst, or even Tulsa. It's a lovely backyard in Oklahoma City, where raised perennial beds enclose a formal lawn and fountain.

perennials weather Central Oklahoma conditions, Warren built raised beds with drain lines in the bottom. He also replaced the original alkaline, hard red clay with a mixture of topsoil and organic matter. Periodic topdressing of the soil with cottonseed meal helps to further acidify it as well as feed the plants.

Gardening has become a never-ending adventure for the Balyeats. "We're always learning, but we still don't know much," Marilyn admits with a laugh. One important thing that they have discovered is which perennials will stomach the sudden freezes, searing heat, ceaseless wind, and parching droughts of Oklahoma City. Their top performers include Shasta daisies, daylilies, black-eyed Susans, pink and yellow yarrow, and blue and white balloon flowers.

Hal and Marilyn's garden should make all citizens of their fair city proud. To say nothing of the dog. ◇

This fountain, given to Hal by his father, now takes center stage.

Lilies
ALMOST HEAVEN

Grow them for their beauty. Grow them for their fragrance. But grow them. They're easy.

BY LINDA C. ASKEY
PHOTOGRAPHY VAN CHAPLIN

Asiatic hybrid lilies, such as this yellow Connecticut King, are ideal for adding height to flower borders.

For gardeners, the streets of heaven will not be lined with gold. We'll have lilies. And they will be as tall as we are, with flowers at eye level and fragrance that perfumes the celestial air.

However, by making the right choices in life we can have heaven here on earth, and that includes lilies in our gardens. Lilies are a point of pride, but they are not as difficult to grow as you might think. Selecting the ones adapted for your area will ensure your success.

Probably the most familiar lily to gardeners and nongardeners alike is the

Easter lily *(Lilium longiflorum)*. What most people don't know is that they make wonderful garden flowers after they have finished blooming. Rather than tossing them in the trash, set them in your garden. They'll bloom the next year from late spring to early summer. Easter lilies are a favorite in the Lower and Coastal South, even where they are exposed to salt spray. Look for new hybrids such as the pink Casa Rosa.

After Easter lilies, the most recognizable lily is probably Stargazer. This crimson beauty is the best known of

The colorful trumpets of Aurelian hybrid lilies make early summer a triumph over spring. These are called Pink Perfection.

the **Oriental hybrids.** With remarkably fragrant flowers measuring up to 10 inches across, this group of lilies can also grow quite tall, some typically reaching 36 to 60 inches. The heavy, waxy petals curve backward and are freckled with color. Others to look for are Casa Blanca, Kyoto, and La Reve. Oriental hybrids grow well in the Upper, Middle, and Lower South, especially where the soil is acid and rich.

Early flowering and hardy, the **Asiatic hybrids** offer the greatest variation, with a wide color range. The most recognizable names include Connecticut King (yellow) and Enchantment (orange); these lilies are often bought by color rather than name and selection. The darker colors seem to have the greatest vigor; these grow best in the Middle and Upper South.

Easter lilies

Stargazer is a popular selection among the Oriental hybrid lilies. As a group, these offer spectacular flowers and fragrance in the garden.

Turk's cap lily (Lilium tenuifolium) *sports a mass of vivid blossoms on 24- to 30-inch stems.*

Beautifully combined, these Asiatics are up to their necks in daisies.

The **Aurelian hybrids,** descended from *L. henryi* (another good lily for the South), are reliable performers. They have trumpet-shaped blooms in a wide range of colors. Pink Perfection, Golden Splendor, and African Queen are garden favorites. These are best for the Middle and Upper South.

For old-fashioned charm and toughness, you can't beat **tiger lilies** (*L. lancifolium,* formerly *L. tigrinum*). They are usually orange, although white, yellow, and red forms are available. Their nodding blooms curl backward in a classic turk's-cap lily form. It grows happily in the Upper, Middle, and Lower South.

The **Formosa lily** (*L. formosanum*) is beloved for its late blooming habit, flowering in August and beyond, when so many other flowers have passed. And it thrives in the Coastal South where many cold-hardy bulbs fail. The big, white trumpets are reminiscent of the Easter lily, but the stalks grow up to 7 feet tall. Seeds sown one year will probably be in bloom the next. Grow them for late-summer blooms throughout the South.

Regal lilies (*L. regale*) grow 4 to 6 feet tall, and the flowers have yellow throats and a blush of pink on the back of the bloom. Resembling Easter lilies, regal lilies will thrive in the Upper, Middle, and Lower South.

The **Madonna lily** (*L. candidum*) is somewhat different than other lilies. Sprouting a winter-hardy rosette of foliage in the fall, it blooms in spring and then goes dormant for the summer. Unlike the other bulbs mentioned, this one is best planted shallowly, with only an inch of soil covering its surface. Given some shade from the afternoon sun, it will grow throughout the South. Gardeners with alkaline soil should note that it is a good choice.

LIFE LESSONS FOR LILIES
Plant bulbs in well-drained soil. If you can put them on a sloping bed, that will help. Otherwise, amend your soil with equal parts compost and sand. The ideal is to have the base of the bulb sitting on a dry material such as sand or gravel, so that the roots reach through that layer into nutrient-rich soil. Set bulbs at a depth about twice the height of the bulb. If the bulb is 3 inches tall, the top of it should be 6 inches underground.

Because lilies are tall and narrow, plant clusters of at least five. More would be even better. If your bulbs never seem to come up, you could have a problem with mice or voles. Plant bulbs in a cage made of berry baskets or hardware cloth.

This is a great time to buy lilies. The bulbs are often at half price, and that's a good buy if they are firm with no sign of rot.

Most lilies need to be staked so that they do not topple over during a summer rain. Be sure to place the stake far enough away from the base of the plant so you don't injure the bulb. ◇

(For sources see pages 250–251.)

Tiger lilies are among the hardiest lilies for the Southern garden. Although typically orange, there are white, yellow, and red forms available.

Though regal lilies bloom happily in our Southern gardens, they were first discovered in China almost a century ago.

*White caladiums and impatiens
(See page 153.)*

July

Summer's Jewel

If ever there were a relationship made in heaven, it is between butterflies and butterfly bush.

In the eyes of a butterfly, nothing is more alluring than the jewel-toned blooms of butterfly bush. And for the gardener looking for certain success, nothing is easier to grow. It begins its flowering season as summer days stretch out. At home in the landscape or at the back of a perennial border, its graceful shape and elongated, slightly fragrant blooms are a constant source of color throughout the summer. And with the first bloom, the butterflies come.

Butterfly bush *(Buddleia davidii)* is a fast-growing, woody-stemmed shrub that requires well-drained soil and full sun. It is rarely disturbed with insect or disease problems. The most active growth spurt is during the spring, when it will attain its maximum height for the year. Once blooming begins in early summer, it will continue until the first frost.

Some occasional maintenance is required to keep flowers flowing. Old blossoms should be removed as they begin to fade and dry. Cut directly above a set of leaves at the base of the flower, and new buds will soon follow.

Bouquets are a colorful, lightly scented addition to a summer table. Clip the woody stems at an angle early in the morning, and place them in water immediately. When you are ready to arrange, make a new cut at a wide angle to allow more exposed surface to be in contact with the water.

Steve Thomas, a wholesale grower with Greene Hill Nursery in Waverly,

(Above) *1. Empire Blue 2. White Bouquet 3. Sungold 4. Pink Delight 5. Bonnie* **(Right)** *Miss Ellen*

BY ELLEN RILEY ■ PHOTOGRAPHY VAN CHAPLIN

Graceful Passage

This garden changes with the seasons of life, as well as the seasons of the year.

BY ORENE STROUD HORTON
PHOTOGRAPHY JEAN ALLSOPP

Not many people begin a garden redo by removing a swimming pool, but Trisha and Charles McCallum of Columbia, South Carolina, did just that.

The McCallum children had enjoyed the pool when they were growing up, but a nearby pecan tree had created a maintenance nightmare. Tired of fishing leaves and pecans out of the pool, Trisha and Charles concluded there was no sense in living with something that they didn't use anymore.

Trisha had collected pictures of gardens, gates, and walls for several years. Both she and Charles knew what they wanted, which is the first step in any good garden. Top on their list was that it should look as good when seen from the house as when standing in its midst. Trisha likes to introduce visitors to the garden from inside her house before she takes them outside. The views change as you go from kitchen to breakfast room to dining room to family room. Trisha's favorite is from the kitchen "because I spend so much time at the sink. We had the windows lowered to open up the view."

After breaking through the sides of the pool to allow for drainage, they had it filled with soil. Old brick edging around the pool became a border for a new rectangle of grass. Trisha suggested placing a fountain behind the new lawn. Charles agreed, reasoning that "water is nice, but you don't need a pool to have it."

The McCallums consulted with garden designer Diane Warren of Sterling Garden Center in Columbia, South Carolina, who drew their ideas to scale. "She recommended some changes that were really important," says Trisha, "such as

A focal point of a garden path, this classically designed storage house blends with the formality of the site.

A lush border of perennials framed by brick-columned entries is a feature of the main garden lawn.

the use of Korean boxwood in a curving hedge behind the new Pan fountain." Diane also reminded them to align new walks with a part of the house so the garden would look as if it had always been there. The McCallums stayed involved, often making little changes as the plan progressed—a different curve to a bed here, another material there.

With no time schedule in mind, Trisha and Charles began the garden renovation in March. A month later, their daughter, Lucia, became engaged and told her mother she would love to hold the wedding reception in the garden. After a moment of panic, Trisha asked if the wedding could wait until the following April. Suddenly, a leisurely paced project acquired a deadline that could not be extended. Masonry work began in June and was completed in August. "Then we had to come in and plant the garden," says Trisha. They had just seven months.

A grassy slope leading from the former pool to the rear of the property was terraced by building a low brick wall. The new wall made the perfect background for a perennial border. Two white Natchez crepe myrtles fit into niches beside the new steps and frame the garden. The Korean boxwood hedge and another of Needlepoint Chinese holly separate the two main garden areas and provide strong evergreen structure in winter.

New garden walls on each side of the property are made of recessed panels of stucco and brick columns. "We modeled them after a wall in Georgetown, South Carolina, that we have always admired," says Trisha. The new wall on the left

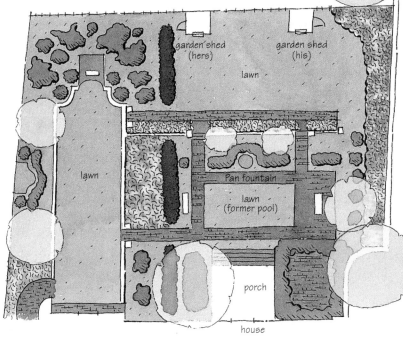

(Above) A fountain provides an appealing break for an expanse of wall. (Left) This Lutyens bench faces another one across the small lawn.

The fig vine-covered steps to the porch are lined with big containers of pink impatiens.

needed something to break up its long expanse. Another fountain seemed the perfect solution. This time they chose a wall fountain that splashes into a pool.

In the shade of pecan and oak trees, the garden brims with hydrangeas, ferns, and cool white impatiens. The new perennial borders offer exciting possibilities for planting in the sun.

As with all renovations, redoing one thing usually makes something else look out of place. The old metal storage shed in the back corner had to go. After Trisha tried unsuccessfully to find another shed she liked, she called Allen Marshall of Architrave in Columbia to design one. Allen suggested they build two sheds. This led to the creation of the delightful his-and-her storage houses, which became features in their new garden. "There were some areas at the rear of the property that needed screening, and two houses with a picket fence behind them was our solution," says Allen.

Charles and his future son-in-law, Bill Smith, did all the construction on the buildings except the stucco. To save time they used standard windows. Although the buildings measure only 6 feet square,

they are well organized inside and hold all the McCallums' garden equipment. Trisha says she can't imagine the backyard without them. "They're not big enough for guesthouses," admits Charles. "But they would make nice playhouses for grandchildren someday," adds Trisha.

Lots of small touches add to the success of the new garden. Behind the storage houses, Charles installed prefab picket fencing and painted it Charleston green. With an existing cherry laurel hedge behind it, it practically disappears. The fence conceals the service area as well as a potting bench he added for Trisha.

In case you're wondering whether they met their deadline, the answer is— just barely. Charles and Bill worked frantically but had to call in some extra help for the crowning touch—the cedar-shake roofs atop the garden houses. On the big day, April showers threatened to drench the garden reception. However, just before the guests arrived, the weather turned nice and everything came off beautifully. Displaying the mix of sunny optimism and rock-hard determination every gardener needs, Trisha smiles and says, "It just had to work out." ◇

Zinnias (See pages 166–168.)

August

Checklist for August

EDITORS' NOTEBOOK

Guess what happened to my neighbor's lawn. No, it wasn't the dog. And no, a fleet of tiny alien spacecraft didn't take off during the night. What happened was that a well-intentioned individual, Herbie Cide (I've changed the name to protect the ignorant), saw nutgrass sprouting in a Bermuda grass lawn and decided to fix it. He spot treated the nutgrass with Roundup, without first checking the label. If he had, he'd have discovered that Roundup is a nonselective weedkiller—it kills *all* grasses, not just nutgrass. Was Herbie's spot treatment effective? You bet! Now my neighbor has nice brown spots all over his lawn. Fortunately, I have the perfect solution—a can of bright green spray paint. Yes, as I tell everyone who will listen, there is hardly a gardening problem in the world that a can of green spray paint won't cure.

Steve Bender

☐ **Bougainvillea**—Train wayward stems of bougainvillea to guide them onto a trellis or fence. Use dark green twine or twist ties to hold the new growth in place. Tie loosely as not to choke the stems.

☐ **Harvest**—Begin your dinner by taking a basket to the garden to see what is ripe and ready. Fresh-picked vegetables always taste best, and nature's plenty is good inspiration for the family cook.

☐ **Lawns**—Avoid close mowing during the hottest season. There is no need to bag clippings if you cut the lawn often enough to keep them from accumulating. Clippings left in place nourish the soil and reduce the need for nitrogen fertilizer.

☐ **Water**—Plants that berry, such as yaupon, burford hollies, and pyracantha, need water to ensure a good crop of fruit this fall. Azaleas and camellias set their buds in late summer and also benefit from deep watering now and during fall dry periods.

PLANT

☐ **Annuals**—Continue to set out transplants of warm-weather annuals to fill the gaps of color this fall. Marigolds, zinnias, celosias, begonias, and geraniums can provide blooms until frost. Water well the first few days after transplanting, and then weekly as needed.▶

☐ **Beach**—Add textural interest to a beach landscape with bird-of-paradise or pampas grass. These plants tolerate conditions on the leeward side of a home where they are protected from the wind and direct salt spray. To be assured of fluffy plumes, buy pampas grass when it is in bloom. Male plants produce thinner plumes, and you won't know which is which until it flowers.

☐ **Bluebonnets**—Broadcast and rake seeds of Texas bluebonnets, Indian paintbrush, coreopsis, and other spring-flowering wildflowers in beds; water thoroughly. The seeds will sprout and develop deep root systems during the fall and winter for blooms next spring.

◀ **Daylilies and irises**—Dig established clumps and divide individual plants. This can rejuvenate plantings that have been in place for several years and provide extra plants to place in your garden or share with friends and neighbors.

☐ **Fall flowers**—Start seeds of favorite biennials and other fall-planted flowers in 4-inch pots. Seedlings will be ready to transplant in the fall. Those easy to start from seed include foxglove, poppies, hollyhock, larkspur, wallflowers, and Canterbury-bells.

☐ **Mums**—When you see mums for sale this month, buy them while the buds are still tight. Plant them in your garden or in containers where they will have maximum impact. Getting mums started early will mean a more natural appearance and longer-lasting color when they bloom. ▶

☐ **Rain lilies**—Dig and divide plants that are too crowded to bloom. Separate clumps, removing and replanting the biggest bulbs about 6 inches apart. The smaller bulbs will take about a year to bloom if replanted.

☐ **Replant**—If the long, hot summer has left flower, herb, and vegetable beds looking tired and bedraggled, replant. Pull out everything that has passed its prime, and assess what you have left. Fill in with a few new summer annuals or add fall vegetables. They'll last until autumn, giving you several months of pleasure.

◀ **Vegetables**—It's time to plan and plant your fall garden, at least in the Middle and Upper South. Turnips, collards, mustard greens, broccoli, lettuce, English peas, garlic, and carrots can all be planted now. In the Lower South, wait until the latter part of this month or the beginning of next month.

This is the last month to start warm-weather vegetables such as tomatoes, okra, squash, and peppers in the Coastal South. The plants need mulch and plenty of water to get them through the hot months.

PRUNE

☐ **Annuals**—Renew summer annuals a final time before fall. Pinch leggy marigolds, cut back or replant zinnias, and remove browned blooms from scarlet sage. Feed plants with a liquid fertilizer such as 20-20-20 to encourage growth for fall.

☐ **Roses**—A light pruning in mid-August helps stimulate an abundance of fall flowers on everblooming, modern, and old garden roses. Remove dead wood; then cut back current season's growth about one-third. Apply 5-10-10 or rose fertilizer as directed on the label or ½ cup cottonseed meal per plant; water thoroughly.

CONTROL

☐ **Roses**—Continue regular Funginex sprays as directed on the label for roses that are susceptible to diseases.

☐ **Weeds**—If annual bluegrass and other winter weeds were a problem in your lawn last spring, you will have to contend with them again unless you control them this fall. The seeds are sitting there waiting to germinate this month. Apply a pre-emergence herbicide such as balan now to stop the problem before it starts.

FERTILIZE

☐ **Compost**—Anytime you prepare a bed for replanting, be sure to include plenty of compost, composted manure, or other organic matter. This will keep clay soil loose, sandy soil moist, and add nutrients at the same time.

☐ **Mulch**—Renew mulch in beds. Finely ground pine bark is a good choice for poor, sandy soil. It doesn't last as long as cypress, pine straw, or bark nuggets, but it will enrich the soil more quickly as it decomposes.

☐ **Orchids**—Orchids potted in bark need more fertilizer than those in osmunda fiber or potting soil because the wood needs more nitrogen as it decomposes. Be sure to feed them regularly with a liquid orchid food diluted according to label directions.

August notes:

TIP OF THE MONTH

Last year, to make sure my houseplants would be okay while I was away on vacation, I soaked a heavy bath towel, put it in the bottom of the bathtub, and placed my plants on top of it. When I returned home a week later, the towel was still damp and the plants were fine.

NITA BRYANT JAMES
LAURINBURG, NORTH CAROLINA

Zinnias say

summertime

in brilliant

bouquets.

carnival
of color

Zinnias are the epitome of ease. A package of seeds and a touch of TLC promise a garden full of old-fashioned flowers begging to be cut. Seed them directly into the soil now, and harvest bouquets this fall until frost.

In Birmingham, Nona Hurst has been growing zinnias *(Zinnia elegans)* for cutting since 1986. Nona saw her first zinnia garden in full summer bloom while on a visit to hometown friend Sarah Whitson, in Talladega, Alabama. She returned home with seeds in hand.

"After planting the seeds from Sarah's garden, I was hooked," she says. "From my first small garden, I took over my husband John's vegetable garden. Now I've got a quarter acre of zinnias planted, and I think that's probably enough." Nona shares with friends and is a well-known supplier to local florists.

While very few of us would undertake such a huge endeavor, Nona's techniques for planting apply to even the smallest garden.

BY ELLEN RILEY
PHOTOGRAPHY
VAN CHAPLIN

The bright blooms of zinnias pair nicely with orange cosmos for a long-lasting summer arrangement.

Zinnias are annuals—they must be planted every year. You can plant them as soon as the last frost has passed in spring. The soil is warm from the summer sun, so seeds germinate quickly. To prepare the flowerbed, turn the soil and add compost. Rake smooth and break up clumps of soil. Make a small trench ½ inch deep in which to drop seeds. Lightly cover with soil, and water thoroughly. Space the rows of seeds 1 foot apart.

When they're several inches tall, thin the seedlings to space the plants 6 inches apart. Thin by gently pulling the extras, or pinch them off at the base. Nona feeds the new seedlings with an all-purpose liquid fertilizer such as 20-20-20.

The summer heat makes the new zinnias grow quickly. When they have grown their first set of true leaves (the ones that look like real zinnia leaves), feed them with a granular time-release fertilizer such as 12-6-6.

Zinnias for cutting grow tall and must be given support to prevent them from falling over. Instead of supporting each plant individually, stake them as a group. Green bamboo plant stakes and twine can be used to make a nearly invisible support. Place bamboo stakes 18 inches apart surrounding the flowerbed. Wind the twine between the stakes to create a grid for the zinnias to grow up through.

The only potential problem these flowers face is powdery mildew. This leaf fungus is a fact of life with zinnias, but there are several methods of prevention. By seeding in late summer, you'll find mildew is less prevalent due to re-duced rainfall and lower humidity in most areas of the South.

Providing good air circulation around plants is also an effective way to prevent mildew. When seeding and thinning, give the plants enough room for air to move easily between them. Water zinnias only when very dry. Use a soaker hose or hose-end sprayer with the stream of water aimed at the base of the plants, with minimal water hitting the leaves. Water in the morning so moisture on the leaves will dry with the heat of the sun.

Nona's late-summer planting produces cut flowers until the first frost. As the growing season begins to wind down, she doesn't cut as many flowers; she allows the blossoms to mature into seedheads that hold next year's garden. If you want to continue cutting flowers, you'll have to spring for seeds next year. ◇

(For sources see pages 250–251.)

(Left) *Even the darkest corner is illuminated with the addition of a single well-placed variegated plant such as Morning Light miscanthus.* **(Inset)** *Snow-on-the-mountain grow well in sun or partial shade.*

Whiter Shade of Pale

While the August garden struggles to overcome yet another month of relentless heat, it's time to forget about hot hues. Think cooling whites, silvers, and creams.

It's amazing how refreshing a dab of white can be. When late summer has extinguished the fire of reds and yellows—and even hot pink seems faded—it's a good idea to have a few variegated plants strategically placed in your garden.

Boasting two-tone foliage, variegated plants are the garden's salvation. Pair them with dark green shrubs for maximum impact. Remember, a little variegation goes a long way; too much of a good thing leads to confusion. A single clump of striped grass or one dappled shrub makes a bright accent.

Jo Kellum

(For sources see pages 250–251.)

BRIGHT IDEAS

When shopping for variegated plants, select silvery shades that will make the garden seem cooler.

Common name	Botanical name	Description	Range
snow-on-the-mountain	*Euphorbia marginata*	self-seeding annual	MS, LS
variegated century plant	*Agave americana* Marginata	evergreen succulent	CS
variegated English ivy	*Hedera helix* Glacier	ground cover or container plant	US, MS, LS
variegated hostas	*Hosta* sp.	ground cover	US, MS, LS
variegated Japanese pittosporum	*Pittosporum tobira* Variegata	evergreen shrub	LS, CS
variegated miscanthus	*Miscanthus sinensis* Morning Light	ornamental	AS

AS=All South, CS=Coastal South, LS=Lower South, MS=Middle South, US=Upper South

Once a forgotten remnant of worn lawn, the Loyds' backyard now features a comfortable, secluded terrace. Evergreen plants give structure to the beds while impatiens add a splash of color.

Backyard Benefits

When Eric and Helen Loyd moved into their Decatur, Georgia, home, all they needed to enjoy their backyard was a cup of coffee and a good book. That's because landscape architect Diane Dunaway had worked with the previous owner, Chip Harbaugh, to make a lot of wishes come true in a small space.

"Chip loves to garden," Diane says, "but he also wanted a place he could unwind at the end of the day, read, as well as entertain." The design works so well that the Loyds enjoy it in similar fashion. "Basically it's another room of the house where we hang out and relax," says Helen.

The four-leaf clover-shaped terrace is a private nook, enclosed from the neighbors by a fence and

BEFORE

separated from the drive by two yaupon hollies, the type that grows into small, gray-barked trees.

One arc of the terrace provides footing for a generous swing. With night lighting and outdoor stereo speakers in the garden, the swing is the place to be at day's end or at its beginning.

Another arc leads to the back door, through the pair of yaupons. Even though you can easily see

through the slender trunks, they give a sense of separation that makes the terrace feel secluded, tucked away from the world. On the other side you have the car, the phone, the responsibilities of life. On the terrace you find shade, flowers, the morning paper, and a mug of hot coffee.

The other two arcs of the cloverleaf terrace swing toward the house and away from it. The arc close to the house creates a spot for a favorite chair, as well as a generous planting bed for evergreen shrubs and seasonal flowers. All summer, impatiens provide an embrace of color.

While the first three arcs have a raised-brick edging, the paved edge on the fourth arc is even with the lawn, inviting a stroll. *Linda C. Askey*

A Courtyard Conversion

Writer Nancy Dillon grew up with mountains in her backyard. So moving to a condo in San Antonio was quite an adjustment.

The 8- x 16-foot enclosed patio was stark white and uninviting. Landscape architect Terry Lewis helped Nancy convert the space into a colorful courtyard. He talked Nancy into staining the concrete. Now it's a muted, sandy color.

STAINING CONCRETE

We bought the same stain as Nancy to try this ourselves, using concrete stepping pads as samples. Lithochrome Chemstain by Scofield comes in a variety of colors; we used Padre Brown. Finished colors will vary according to the age, composition, and surface texture of the concrete. The stain produces a chemical reaction when applied, so the color becomes part of the concrete surface.

You can apply a single coat for a light color or more coats for darker tones.

We tried Terry's trick for creating a dark border around the edge of each concrete square—with great results.

Step 1: Wear chemical gloves to apply a single coat of stain to clean concrete with a foam brush. Rub lightly in a circular motion, and don't be alarmed when the stain appears greenish and fizzy.

Step 2: Allow the first coat to dry completely. Mask the square with duct tape, leaving 1½ inches visible at the edges. Apply a second coat to this area. Do not add more stain to the center area.

Step 3: After the second coat is dry, peel duct tape to remove.

Unlike paint that only coats the surface, concrete stain etches the surface, making it lasting and durable. Stain produces mottled colors that age to an attractive patina. One gallon of stain will cover 150 to 200 square feet with a single coat. However, for darker tones, two coats are recommended. *Jo Kellum*

(For sources see pages 250–251.)

This sunken garden in Charleston, South Carolina, is carpeted with Zoysia for a fine-textured finish.

Emerald Islands

The grass is green and the mowing is easy.

Not all lawns provoke yawns. Little patches of grass, crisply edged and neatly shaped, can give your yard a stamp of distinction.

It's easy to grow a pretty postage-stamp lawn. The main thing to consider is the location. To get the most from your little lawn, think of it as an area rug for your yard. Just as a well-placed rug can anchor an intimate conversation area in your living room, the soft surface of a panel of grass can provide the same effect.

Surround your lawn with a hard surface to emphasize its shape and separate it from the other plants in the garden. Paving, cobblestones, or low walls are good ways to outline the shape you want. Avoid the temptation to choose a too-fancy shape; instead, select one that belongs in your garden. ▶

BY JO KELLUM
PHOTOGRAPHY TINA CORNETT,
SYLVIA MARTIN

"The simpler the shape, the better," explains Huntsville, Alabama, garden designer Bill Nance. "If you make a shape that is too complicated, you will call too much attention to the edge of the lawn. An understated lawn that pulls its shape from other structural elements adds serenity to the garden."

Try this design trick: Imagine a pool of water in your garden. The shape and the spot where you would build such a pool are good guidelines for planning your small lawn. Landscape architect Charlotte Goodwyn used this technique when designing her own Montgomery backyard.

"There was a real temptation for me to consider including a garden pool. But with a lot of trees, I decided grass would be easier to rake and blow leaves off of," she explains. "So instead of a pool of water, which I didn't want to maintain, I designed a pool of lawn."

There's another advantage to choosing grass over water: You can walk on it.

> To me, the lawn is like a thick rug that has a pad under it.
>
> *Garden designer Bill Nance*

A panel of lawn will add a cooling color to your garden. It will also reflect less heat than a solidly paved surface. A pond could have a similar effect, but the grass is a good spot for setting up extra chairs for outdoor entertaining.

Good drainage and plenty of sun are necessary for your lawn to thrive. Sculpting the soil before planting grass can improve drainage and make your small lawn more attractive. Crown the soil so that it's slightly higher in the center, causing rainwater to flow away to the sides. "When you've got a flat lawn surrounded by a flat walk, it's like the plains of the Sahara," says Bill. "Grass is like green velvet. It should drape over a cushion for an upholstered appearance."

It's important not to go overboard when you mound the soil. The smaller the lawn, the less soil you need to add. A couple of inches will do the job. Bill says, "Berming just slightly will give your lawn a soft, quilted look." ◇

"It takes longer to get out the lawnmower than to mow the grass. We just run the wheel of the lawnmower around on the surrounding stones; we don't even have to edge the lawn." LANDSCAPE ARCHITECT CHARLOTTE GOODWYN

White star zinnia, ivy, and blue salvia (See pages 182-184.)

September

Quick
AND COLORFUL

Seasonal mums

meet their match

with striking

companions.

Chrysanthemums and fireplugs have a lot in common. They're both stout and sturdy, won't waver in a stiff breeze, and stand perpetually at attention. But what mums may lack in grace, they more than make up for in brilliant blossoms.

Every year there are new chrysanthemum colors introduced. In a world once dominated by yellow, there are now plenty of pink and lavender selections, as well as rich reds and oranges. Flower types can vary too; some chrysanthemum blooms are tight cushions, while others look like daisies.

When planting containers, plan them around a central color scheme. But instead of choosing all one color, use mums in complementary shades or flower types. Add companion plants to loosen up their image. Many of the ones we used are houseplants. Once the mums have finished blooming, repot the companions and bring them indoors for winter.

BY ELLEN RILEY
PHOTOGRAPHY JEAN ALLSOPP,
VAN CHAPLIN

INDOOR AUTUMN

Mums used indoors will last for several weeks. Plants in 4-inch pots are readily available and the perfect size to incorporate into arrangements—pots and all. A chrysanthemum in a small container will need to be watered every few days. Remove the mums from the arrangement, and water in the kitchen sink. Soak thoroughly, and drain well before replacing.

Give your arrangement the unrestrained appearance of the one shown on page 182 with the addition of bromeliads and ferns. A bromeliad's strong, pointed foliage should extend a bit beyond the perimeter of the container. It blooms for several months, making it a good longterm investment. Water only when dry.

(Right) Vibrant bleeding-heart vine is the perfect backdrop for pink and lavender mums in containers dripping with interesting companions.

(Below) White Star zinnia and trailing ivy ramble around mums in a window box. Tall blue salvia towers above.

Assorted asparagus ferns add an airy texture that fills out the arrangement. These ferns are easy to care for. Water them as you do the chrysanthemums.

Gourds, persimmons, pomegranates, and nandina berries all add another dimension. Cluster them on the edge of the container, allowing the berries to cascade over the side. Nandina berries will need to be replaced after several weeks, but the other items will last for a month or more.

OUTDOOR SENSATIONS

The yellow, orange, or red fruit of ornamental peppers is a perfect complement to similarly colored mums. The peppers' small points add a contrasting shape to the mums' fat, round flowers.

Colorful croton is a bit like a chameleon. The multicolored leaves look great with many different mum colors. Croton grows as upright as mums, so the addition of a trailing plant beneath it helps keep the arrangement from becoming too stiff and upright.

The wide, waxy foliage of purple heart *(Setcresea pallida)* adds depth in color and contrast to the large container shown at left. It spills over the pot to create a soft edge. When planted outside, purple heart is perennial in the Lower South. It also roots easily from cuttings and may be brought indoors from year to year.

Pink- and lavender-colored mums bring a different look to fall. Pair them with rex begonia, pink-striped calathea, and tricolor dracaena to achieve the look of the smaller container shown at left. Purple heart and English ivy spilling over the edge complete the combination.

WHICH MUM'S FOR YOU?

Garden mums are compact, flower-covered perennials. After using them in containers, you can plant them in the garden. Remove old blooms before planting. Loosen the tight root ball to help the plant become established. Water well throughout autumn if rainfall is minimal.

Florist or pot mums have larger flowers than garden mums. They have been grown in greenhouses to use indoors and will not return if planted outside. They are most successfully used indoors. ◇

If your garden looks fatigued, give it a dose of horticultural caffeine in the form of new plants for the fall.

Your Garden's Second Chance

Some of you are feeling pretty guilty right now. Either you let your flowers burn up this summer or you never planted any in the first place. Your front yard looks so bleak you're using tumbleweed as an ornamental grass.

Put your conscience on hold. Here's your second chance. Many garden centers restock this month with new shipments of flowering plants. And we're not talking about just the expected, such as pansies, violas, and mums. No, we're talking about all sorts of annuals, perennials, shrubs, and vines.

For example, you may notice your garden center stocking fresh marigolds this fall. Marigolds give you the same yellows, golds, and oranges as garden mums. And if you factor in the longer bloom time of marigolds (from now until frost throughout most of the South and into winter in the Coastal and Tropical South), they cost less than mums.

Have you considered planting petunias for fall? Petunias love autumn weather and offer the blue, violet, and lavender colors marigolds lack. Or try blue mealy-cup sage, sweet alyssum, and lantana. They'll all bloom continuously until a

Marigolds are a good choice for long-lasting color in the garden.

hard freeze (and throughout winter where it doesn't freeze). For a knockout display to wow your neighbors, you can't beat the spectacular purple-and-white flowers of Mexican bush sage.

Now is the time to look for pots of fall-blooming perennials. Asters of course lead the pack, but don't overlook such autumn all-stars as Japanese anemone, ginger lily, Autumn Joy sedum, and ornamental grasses. As for shrubs, many roses get their second wind in September, blooming better than they have for months. You'll also enjoy the late-season blooms of butterfly bush, Blue Mist caryopteris, tardiva hydrangea, and Confederate rose *(Hibiscus mutabilis).*

Adding tropical shrubs and vines to your fall garden may seem crazy if you live where it freezes in winter. But you can always bring tropicals inside when it's time. The great advantage they offer is nearly nonstop blooming. Keep an eye out for Chinese hibiscus, mandevilla, allamanda, yellow shrimp plant, and Egyptian starclusters *(Pentas lanceolata).*

But don't wait too long. You only get one last chance. *Steve Bender*

SHOPPING LIST FOR FALL

SHRUBS
Blue Mist caryopteris—blue, purple flowers
butterfly bush—fragrant blue, purple, pink, white flowers
Confederate rose—pink, red, white flowers
Roses—many colors
Tardiva hydrangea—white flowers

TROPICALS
Allamanda (vine)—yellow flowers
Bougainvillea—pink, red, purple, white flowers
Chinese hibiscus—red, yellow, salmon, pink, orange flowers
Egyptian starclusters—red, pink, white flowers
Mandevilla (vine)—pink flowers
Yellow shrimp plant—yellow flowers

ANNUALS
Coleus—multicolored foliage
Lantana—yellow, red, orange, white flowers*
Marigold—yellow, gold, orange, red flowers
Mealy-cup sage—blue, white flowers*
Mexican bush sage—purple-and-white flowers*
Petunia—flowers of almost every color
Sweet alyssum—white, pink, purple flowers*
* Hardy in areas with mild winters

PERENNIALS
Asters—blue, purple, red, pink, white flowers
Autumn Joy sedum—rose flowers
Cardinal flower—red flowers
Ginger lily—white flowers
Goldenrod—yellow flowers
Japanese anemone—white, pink, red flowers
Ornamental grasses—white, tan, pink plumes

PHOTOGRAPHS: SYLVIA MARTIN / GARDEN DESIGN: TOM PELLETT, MEMPHIS

You'd never guess how close this cozy backyard is to the neighbor's house.

Favorite Place

Transforming a cramped back-yard into a comfortable outdoor room made a new house feel more like home for a Memphis couple. Previously, French doors opened to a narrow garden spot with views of the house next door.

Today, 8-foot priva-cy fencing screens the view and separates the backyard from the ad-jacent parking court. Lattice gateways at each end of the area help keep breezes flowing through the narrow space.

The deck hugs the house, making the most of every square inch. The homeowners have supper there nearly

An architectural relic transforms a blank brick wall.

every evening until winter. There's also plenty of room for guests.

A brick-on-sand walk, laid in a basket-weave pattern, leads from the parking court to the deck. Planting beds on each side of the walk are just large enough for puttering. "We are empty nesters, and we travel a lot," says the homeowner. "But we love doing the plant-ing, weeding, and fer-tilizing. This is just the right size for gardening without being tied down to a lot of land."

The plants were chosen to thrive in the restricted space. Akebia swarms over a wooden archway, and a climb-

Mexican bush sage steals the show in the reverse view. The wooden arch serves as the entrance.

ing rose decorates the fence. Foster's hollies, sweet bay magnolias, a Japanese maple, and a tree-form yaupon holly all add height without taking over. Low-growing plants such as Bath's Pink dianthus, Au-tumn Joy sedum, sweet flag, and variegated liriope edge the beds.

The small backyard is just right for this family. It's their favorite place to be. *Jo Kellum*

Simple geometric forms based on classical proportion and scale instill formality to the structures.

An 18-inch-high ledge defines the front of the pool. A cascading fountain flanked by landscaped beds provides a focal point.

The pool pavilions and adjacent garage were positioned to frame views from the living room.

Pristine Pavilions

Folly, according to Webster, is "an often extravagant picturesque building erected to suit a fanciful taste." *Everyman's Concise Encyclopaedia of Architecture* defines it as "a useless building, erected on the grounds of a wealthy eccentric, especially in the 18th and early 19th centuries."

Although the wonderful addition behind Robert and Denise Gorham's Bethesda, Maryland, home might be considered a folly by some, their gem in the garden is hardly useless. It's as practical as it is pretty.

"My husband wanted a garage, and I wanted a pool," says Denise. "That's how the whole project got started." But the Gorhams didn't have a lot of room to work with—their backyard is 50 feet wide with an angled depth of 70 to 100 feet.

Undaunted by the dimensions, architect Stephen Vanze of Barnes Vanze & Associates manipulated classical scale and proportion to make the most of the situation. He aligned the pool on axis with the living room French doors.

To create an illusion of depth, two square pavilions housing changing rooms and a small kitchenette anchor the far end of the pool. The configuration of the lot allowed for the garage to step back so the two pavilions could serve as freestanding objects in the landscape.

Their forms are classic, but the size of each pavilion is actually based on practical concerns. "Each is just large enough to accommodate a standard door with a bench and counter on either side," says Stephen.

A 42-inch-high curving wall of stacked fieldstone embraces the two pavilions. This rounded niche provides a spot for a whirlpool spa. A flagstone terrace surrounds the pool and carves out a space for a small grass lawn. Stacked-stone walls beside the pool frame beds for a variety of annual and perennial plants.

Denise confesses she was not a gardener before. "We had no idea it would turn out so well and be so easy to maintain," she says. "Throughout the year it's simple to add pots with color. And when there's a weed, it's so obvious that I run out and pull it immediately." *Lynn Nesmith*

flower & *water*

BY STEVE BENDER
PHOTOGRAPHY ALLEN ROKACH

Blessed relief—that's the operative term for this pool and garden in St. Michaels, Maryland. Whether you're in the water doing the backstroke or simply admiring the scene from the house, you can't help but notice how *comfortable* everything feels.

The credit goes to two people—landscape designer Jan Kirsh Alspach of Bozman, Maryland, and building designer Clint Wadsworth of Royal Oak. Their handiwork beautifully unites flower and water, leaf and shelter. It also addresses the lay of the land, taking in scenic views while blocking the unpleasant ones. Most importantly, its modest scale and natural appearance immediately put you at ease.

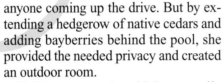

This combination of butterfly bush, Russian sage, and purple heart reflects the owners' color preference.

It's hard to imagine a prettier site for a pool than this one, which gazes longingly toward San Domingo Creek on Maryland's Eastern Shore. Problem was, environmental rules forbade placing a pool at the most logical spot, between the house and creek. This forced Jan to locate it in the front yard in full view of

Ornamental grasses mulched with gravel and stones lend an Oriental touch. "I was trying to create something interesting texturally," says the landscape designer.

anyone coming up the drive. But by extending a hedgerow of native cedars and adding bayberries behind the pool, she provided the needed privacy and created an outdoor room.

Unlike most pools, which are totally divorced from the rest of the yard, this one enjoys the close embrace of flowers, grasses, shrubs, and vines. But Jan made sure her plantings framed a view of the creek and didn't hide it. As you look from the pool house toward the pool's far end, you notice that bluestone pavers form a point. This feature draws your eye through an opening in the trees out to the creek beyond.

The pool's most refreshing element is its homey, understated pool house. No massive marble columns or Palladian

The plan labels: planting bed, pool house, pavilion, honeysuckle, driveway, spa, gravel, planting bed, pool, lawn, walk, to creek, house

windows here; instead, you discover something cozy, much more like a cottage. "I tried to capture the flavor of the Eastern Shore," says Clint, "relaxed, comfortable, and unassuming. We didn't want the house to fight the landscape. The landscape should be dominant."

Jan agrees. "The pool house was designed for family and friends," she says, "not a country club."

But what's that green thing sprouting from the roof? Answer—trumpet honeysuckle *(Lonicera sempervirens)*. Clint had added a small pavilion to the pool house, then left open a section of pressure-treated rafters to act as a trellis. Now the lush vines underscore the link between house and garden. He explains, "Oftentimes, plant support structures

What makes this garden so pleasant? Start with a pool house that looks like a cottage. Then add water surrounded by colorful plants.

look like they've just been plastered onto a building. The idea here was to have the house and structure work together."

According to Jan, this project marks that rare instance when a "dream design" came true. "When I did the original plans for the garden, I did four versions, showing what I could do with the space," she recalls. "The one the owners actually chose was the most far-out, the biggest stretch artistically. So when they called me back and said, 'Let's go for number four,' I was really thrilled."

You could say their answer was blessed relief. ◇

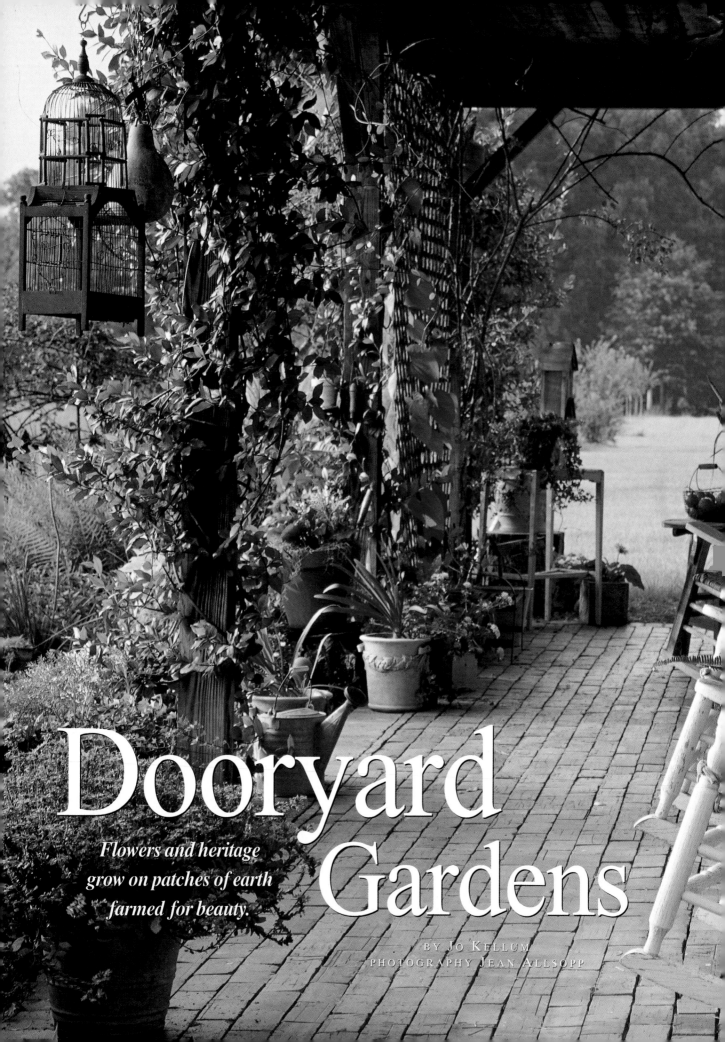

Dooryard
Gardens

*Flowers and heritage
grow on patches of earth
farmed for beauty.*

BY JO KELLUM
PHOTOGRAPHY JEAN ALLSOPP

Set among the flowers, Chippendale chairs contrast with a feed silo.

The seedlings of Southern gardening sprouted bravely in the rich, black dirt of yesterday's scattered farms. Brave because chickens scratched out seeds, goats nipped off buds, and heaven knows what destruction a loose cow could wreak. But the women who planted these gardens were equipped with the patience of farmers' wives who know crop failure up close and personal. And it was the women who, by and large, desired the gardens, hoed plots of earth, and tended them.

Kitchen gardens earned their keep. Food on the table was their obvious justification. But carved indulgently from farmland and squared neatly at the door—that was the spot for flowers. Plants grew for no other reason but prettiness.

The original dooryard garden required no real planning. A fence was essential to keep cows and flower-mashing dogs out, and the design was dictated by the need for a path to the door. Bisected with mirrorlike precision, the symmetry was born of practicality—a straight-line path being the shortest route to the door. The garden grew up on either side of this axis like hair parted in the middle.

Fencing in a garden by the door is still a useful way to define space and

create an intimate area on a large lot. Colorful flowers are located by tradition near the front door, calling attention to a home's entry.

Jim and Len Horne's dooryard garden in Albany, Georgia, is the real thing. A barn converted into a weekend cabin is at home on 75 acres of pastureland and cypress swamps.

Len's mother and grandmother were both gardeners; she followed in their footsteps. "We went to the farm each day for Jim to tend the cows, and I wanted a project. I knew I wanted to plant some color, so I pored over books and magazines for garden ideas."

Next Jim sprayed the area in front of the cabin to kill the grass and weeds. The cows contributed compost, and Len started sun-loving plants such as Queen Anne's lace,

buddleia, coneflowers, coleus, zinnias, and salvias.

Today, a grass path leads straight to the front door, dividing two beds of bright flowers. Butterflies and hummingbirds inspect the garden daily in summer. Jim and Len visit regularly to weed, water, and putter. Hemmed in by the fence, the flowers in their care flourish, growing for no reason but prettiness. ◇

(Above) *Divided by a wide grass path leading to the door, this South Georgia dooryard garden is at home in front of a barn-turned-cabin.*

Red maple
(See pages 202–204.)

October

Checklist
for
October

EDITORS' NOTEBOOK

If there's a showier plant in fall than Mexican bush sage *(Salvia leucantha),* it must be hiding on Mars. But even jaded gardeners on the Angry Red Planet would be impressed with this salvia. I set out a 1-gallon plant in spring; by fall, it's a shrub 4 feet tall and wide with spectacular flowers. Many Lower South gardeners claim it overwinters. But I've never gotten it to come back. After investigation, I've concluded a return depends on excellent drainage; winter temperatures above 15 degrees; a relatively dry autumn and winter; mulching with pine straw after a hard freeze; and growing the all-purple form instead of purple-and-white. If this is too demanding, buy a new plant each spring. Or sign up for the next Martian horticultural tour and discover what they've really stashed in those canals.

Steve Bender

☐ **Bulbs**—Tulips, hyacinths, ranunculus, anemones, and spring starflower *(Iphieon uniflorum)* should all be purchased now for spring color. If you live in the Lower or Coastal South, chill tulips and hyacinths for six weeks in the vegetable bin of your refrigerator prior to planting.

☐ **Chrysanthemums**—For a longer fall show, select plants that still have many unopened buds. As flowers fade, pinch them off. Many times new buds will form.

☐ **Compost**—If you don't have a compost pile, now is a good time to start one. All you need is an enclosure such as a ring of wire fencing or a bin manufactured for the purpose. Add leaves, vegetable trimmings from the kitchen, spent annuals, and grass clippings. Exclude any diseased plants or weeds with seeds.

☐ **Dried flowers**—Pick stems of globe amaranth, zinnias, and cockscomb; dry by hanging stems upside down in a well-ventilated garage or attic for two to three weeks. Harvest gourds now and allow them to dry several weeks before using.

☐ **Houseplants**—Before bringing your tropical foliage plants back indoors, check to see if they need repotting. They grow surprisingly fast during the summer. Also check for insects such as scale or mealybugs. It is easier to spray while they are still outdoors. Apply SunSpray horticultural oil or Orthene as directed on the label.

☐ **Ground covers**—This is a good time to plant beds of ground covers. Divide clumps of liriope and mondo grass into small pieces, each containing some roots. That way you can get 6 to 10 plants from a single pot.

☐ **Daffodils**—It's months away, but this is the time to plan and plant for spring. Buy spring-flowering bulbs, such as daffodils, while the selection is good. If you can't find good selections locally, there's still time to mail-order. Place them in well-drained beds that receive at least a half-day of direct sunlight. Selections such as Ice Follies, Golden Dawn, Erlicheer, and Silver Chimes are readily available. ▶

☐ **Flowers**—Impatiens, marigolds, ageratum, verbena, and geraniums love the warm days and cool nights of Coastal South winters. Set these out now

with a dose of time-release fertilizer (9-9-6 or 11-40-6) to keep them blooming.

◀ **Flower seeds**—In the Lower South, it's time to sow seeds of bachelor's-buttons, poppies, larkspur, Johnny-jump-ups, nasturtiums, drummond phlox, stock, and sweet peas directly into a well-prepared bed. Seedlings that develop through winter make stronger plants than those started in spring.

☐ **Flower transplants**—Sweet alyssum, calendula, candytuft, pansy, petunia, snapdragon, and viola transplants are readily available. Purchase and plant them now for months of color.

◀ **Herbs**—Remember to start dill, fennel, chervil, and cilantro from seed now. Sow directly into sunny, prepared beds. Thin to 4 to 6 inches apart. When plants reach full size, cut back the flavorful foliage regularly.

□ **Perennials**—This is the ideal time to plant perennials. They'll have months to develop roots to support new growth that begins again next spring.

□ **Salad greens**—Sow several different selections of leaf lettuce directly into rich, loose soil. Don't bury the seeds. Instead, sprinkle them on top of the ground and water daily until seedlings sprout. You might consider buying transplants in the Middle and Upper South for quick results. If an early frost threatens your plants, cover them with an old sheet or use a row cover sold for this purpose. Floating row covers are translucent, so they do not have to be removed for growth to continue. ▶

□ **Tree planting**—Don't let the higher price of a large tree prevent you from planting now; buy a small one, instead. Smaller, young trees often catch up to large ones within two or three years.

□ **Vegetables**—Don't forget that transplants of cabbage, broccoli, cauliflower, and collards can be set out now for late fall and winter harvest. Carrots, radishes, lettuce, mustard, turnips, arugula, French sorrel, and parsley can all be started from seed. These and other cool-weather vegetables and herbs are good choices for containers.

CONTROL

□ **Perennials**—Hardy perennials that have grown out of bounds or have declined due to overcrowding can be divided now. Lift entire clumps of hostas, ferns, lamb's-ears, helianthus, and others. Reset divisions at the depth they were originally growing, and water well.

□ **Pests**—Cabbage loopers and cabbageworms are the bane of the fall garden. If your plants are beginning to look like lace, sprinkle them with *Bacillus thuringiensis,* sold as Thuricide or Dipel. This bacteria will not harm humans, but it will put a stop to these hungry caterpillars.

FERTILIZE

□ **Hardy annuals**—Prepare soil for pansies and violas by working in several inches of organic material along with 2 pounds of slow-release fertilizer such as 9-9-6 per 100 square feet of bed area. Wait until soil and air temperatures have begun to cool before planting; water well if rains are inadequate.

□ **Lawns**—Continue overseeding bare areas and new lawns with annual or perennial ryegrass or a blend such as Super Star at the rate of 4 to 5 pounds per 1,000 square feet. Fertilize newly seeded areas at the rate of 1 pound of actual nitrogen per 1,000 square feet or use slow-release fertilizers according to label instructions. Water well.

□ **Spinach**—For a better harvest this winter, add lime to acid soil. Choose hydrated lime, which works fast, or pelletized lime, which is easier to use and less caustic but needs several weeks to act. Follow your soil test recommendations or package directions for how much to apply. Soak spinach seeds before planting to help them sprout more easily.

October notes:

THE SIMPLE BEAUTY OF
Red Maple

It grows quickly, thrives almost everywhere, and turns glorious colors in fall.

BY STEVE BENDER
PHOTOGRAPHY
VAN CHAPLIN,
ALLEN ROKACH

Stand quietly this autumn morning in the still, cool atmosphere of dawn. Watch spears of sunlight ignite distant red maples, resplendent in raiments of scarlet and gold. It is one of life's transcendent moments—simple, pure, and yours alone.

Widely admired for its beauty, red maple engenders questions too. Why, you wonder, does a tree called "red" sometimes turn yellow, sometimes red, and sometimes a mixture of the two? That's because red maple isn't named for its fall foliage—it's named for ruby-colored flowers that appear in late winter and the scarlet winged seeds that form shortly thereafter.

A truly cosmopolitan tree, red maple *(Acer rubrum)* occurs naturally over the eastern two thirds of the United States, from the Canadian border down to Florida and the Gulf Coast. It adapts to most soils, from acid to alkaline to wet, so it's as good a tree in Texas as it is in Tennessee. In youth, it grows quickly—often more than 2 feet a year—eventually

making an excellent shade tree 50 to 60 feet tall. Its growth speed and accommodating nature endear it to new homeowners who want quick shade from a tree not likely to die.

No tree varies more in autumn than this one. Individuals of yellow-green, bright canary, apricot-orange, and lava-red frequently grow side by side in a single grove. Trees of one color may sport a single branch of another color. Such eccentricity results from a mad scramble of genes responsible for manufacturing different pigments in the leaves.

Most folks prefer scarlet fall color in the maples they plant. There are two ways to procure this. The first is to buy or dig a tree at its peak of fall color. The color you see now will be the color you get later. The second is to plant a named selection chosen for its brilliant red fall color.

Many selections of red maple exist. But there's no

Red maple's name often belies its color. Depending upon the tree's genetic makeup, it may turn yellow, gold, apricot, or orange.

point in discussing most of them, as garden centers usually sell only two—Red Sunset and October Glory. For a comparison, I called an old friend, Mike Dirr, professor of Horticulture at the University of Georgia. Mike confirmed my own observations—for gardeners in the Middle, Lower, and Coastal South, October Glory prevails, hands down.

Although introduced by Princeton Nursery in New Jersey, October

Glory seems to have Southern blood. It thrives in heat, tolerates drought, and turns color quite late—early- to mid-November in Atlanta, Birmingham, Little Rock, and Dallas. Year in and year out, it's a consistent performer turning brilliant, translucent red. Red Sunset, on the other hand, colors earlier, usually turns orange-red, and prefers cooler climes. In the Upper South, it's the equal of October Glory. In the Midwest, it's the champ.

One of the better red maples that deserve wider use is a selection called Autumn Flame. A fast grower, it turns bright red nearly a month earlier than October Glory.

In your yard, you'll find red maple makes a top-notch lawn tree. Its shade isn't so dense you can't grow grass beneath it. It's a fine street tree too, as long as you don't squeeze it between the sidewalk and curb. If you plant a red maple this fall, dig a nice, big hole (at least twice as wide as the root ball), and plant the tree no deeper than the top of its root ball. Mulch it well, and water it regularly the first year. Each fall thereafter, it will serve up transcendent moments—simple, pure, and yours alone. ◇

Leafy Assistance

Pansies dominate flowerbeds across the South each fall. This popular annual is easy to grow and comes in so many different colors, it's no wonder many gardeners rely on it for fall and winter color. For interesting combinations with pansies, select a few foliage plants to assist them in your flowerbeds.

The large, decorative leaves of ornamental cabbage and kale will enhance your pansies. Cabbage has round leaves and kale sports frilly foliage. These thick-leaved, sturdy plants thrive in cool weather, but temperatures in the low 20s will brown their edges; temperatures in the teens can turn them to mush. The outer leaves are usually green, and the inner ones can range in color from pink to purple to white. Foliage grows in an open rosette pattern, resembling a large flower.

These plants can grow about a foot tall and wide. In a border or flowerbed they make a good backdrop for smaller, more delicate plants. They also work nicely in containers. A sunny site with well-drained soil will keep them happy.

Parsley is another foliage plant that can be set out in the fall and combines well with pansies. There are two types of parsley: flat-leaf and curly-leaf. The flat-leaf type is also known as Italian parsley. It has a better flavor than the curly-leaf and is used for cooking. Curly-leaf is more showy and is often used as a garnish.

Both of these plants look outstanding in the garden. The chartreuse foliage glows in the winter when most plants are dormant. It will live through the winter where temperatures don't drop below 15 degrees. Set out transplants in the fall or early spring. Parsley is a biennial growing only foliage the first year, then flowering and going to seed its second year. The first year produces tender, tasty foliage, but by the second year the foliage gets tough and has a bitter, strong taste. This is why many people treat it as an annual and replant it each year.

Parsley prefers a sunny site but will tolerate light shade. Well-drained soil is a must. It grows about a foot tall. To harvest, clip the stems around the outside base of the plant. Frequent clippings will encourage bushier plants.

This fall as you select pansies from your local garden center, look for a few foliage plants to assist them in your flowerbeds and containers. Ornamental cabbage and kale, with their colorful, mounding leaves, make a bold autumn statement. And the bright green foliage of parsley adds a little spice to your garden. ◇

Colorful ornamental kale looks nice with white-and-purple pansies and fallen leaves. Parsley sprigs add a tasty and visual treat.

Luck With Larkspur

I love larkspur. I can't grow larkspur. I am very mad. But rather than take it out on pets, colleagues, and pieces of office furniture, I decided to find out why. I called up Ed Givhan in Montgomery. Ed knows more about growing flowers than Dennis Rodman knows about hair dye.

"So, Ed, what's the secret to growing larkspur?" I asked. "Radioactive potting soil? A pact with the devil?"

"Neither," he says. "I learned all about larkspur from my grandmama. She used to grow larkspur and poppies, and she always planted in mid- to late-fall."

Aha! Secret number one—sow the seeds in fall, preferably in October or November. Ed says they'll germinate in about three weeks, develop good root systems over the winter, and bloom like crazy the next spring.

"How deep should you bury the seeds?" I inquired. "Would 3 to 4 feet be about right?"

"Only if you're a gopher," he replied. "Larkspur seeds need light to germinate. I draw out a little area in the dirt where I want them—usually between other flowers that are blooming in the fall—then just throw out the seeds and barely scratch them in." Sow thickly, so that seedlings come up in clusters—larkspur looks better that way. Don't mulch with pine straw, he cautions. Leave the soil bare or sow on top of a light mulch consisting of finely crushed pine bark.

Excelsior! Secret number two—sow the seeds shallowly and don't entomb them beneath an avalanche of mulch.

Well, Ed, I'm going to try growing larkspur your grandmama's way this fall. Better hope it works. Or I'll be *very* mad. *Steve Bender*

Larkspur resembles delphinium but is better suited to the Southern climate and doesn't need staking. The flowers appear at the same time in spring as those of bearded iris.

This Lily Deserves a Look

Eucharis lily *(Eucharis x grandiflora)* surely qualifies as one of the most elegant indoor plants. Also known by the common name of Amazon lily (a clue to its South American origins), it adds dignity and grace to any setting.

When not in bloom, the plant is a dead ringer (or at least a close cousin) for dracaena. Actually, it's a bulb more closely related to amaryllis than dracaena. Even if it never flowered, this lily would make a good-looking houseplant. Glossy green leaves radiate out from the base, creating a nice, full effect. Two or three bulbs fit just fine in a 10- to 12-inch pot; choose a 6- to 8-inch container if you are planting one bulb. These plants seem to bloom better when they are potbound.

Its nodding white flowers let you know you've got something special. Appearing in spring, summer, or even into late fall, the fragrant blooms rise high above the foliage on graceful green stalks. There can be as many as six (2½-inch-wide) blooms on one stem; as many as three open at the same time. The bloom period lasts several weeks; simply cut the stalk down at its base when the show is over.

You can encourage reblooming by keeping the plant in a sunny window, or set it outdoors under a shade tree or on a covered porch; direct sun could scorch the leaves. Keep the soil on the dry side for several weeks; then begin watering regularly to trigger another bloom cycle.

You can easily get new plants by removing the little bulbs on the outer edge of the large central bulb after flowering.

You'd be hard-pressed to find a houseplant more graceful and attractive than eucharis lily. Clusters of fragrant, white blossoms look down from slender stalks rising above emerald foliage. Plants can bloom several times a year, with as many as six starlike flowers on each stalk.

To do this, set the pot on newspaper and lay it over on its edge. Gently roll the pot from side to side while teasing the plant out of the container. (Grab the plant at the base of the leaves, not their ends.) Repot the new bulbs in sterile potting soil, and give them the same light exposure as the parent plant. Look for these lilies at well-stocked garden centers in early spring. *Mark G. Stith*

(For sources see pages 250–251.)

EUCHARIS LILY
At a Glance

Height: 10 inches (foliage only); 18-24 inches with flower stalk

Light: tolerant of low light once it's in bloom; does better near a sunny window

Water: Keep the soil on the dry side during the cooler months (October-April), evenly moist at other times of the year.

Fertilizer: Use a water-soluble fertilizer such as Miracle-Gro or ProSol every 4-6 weeks.

Expect to pay: about $10 per individual bulb; about $25 or more for a good-size plant in bloom

A weathered bench at the end of a mulched path serves as a destination, drawing you into the garden either physically or visually.

Hidden Treasures

Most entry plantings focus your attention on the front door. But that's not the best strategy in every case. This home in Jacksonville, Florida, shows why.

The house features recessed pockets on either side of the porch. Landscape architect Bob Hartwig took advantage of this by fashioning a pair of tiny gardens that you discover as you near the front steps.

"Our objective was to create a mini garden in each of those pockets that complemented the planting at the front door," explains Bob. "Then we added a bench and some containers that looked old, weathered, and interesting in each area, so you'd have a reason to go into these spaces."

Because the gardens face east, they receive some morning sun but none in the afternoon. So Bob chose a variety of shade-tolerant evergreens, such as nandina, ligustrum, Japanese boxwood, azalea, and mondo grass. It's the blending of different textures and shades of green that catches your eye and moves it throughout these little spaces. The brightest color here comes from the border of Silvery Sunproof liriope that separates these gardens from the lawn.

Designs such as this prove that it's not always best to rush to the door. Take the time to look to the side, lest you miss some hidden treasures. *Steve Bender*

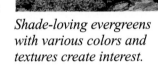

Shade-loving evergreens with various colors and textures create interest.

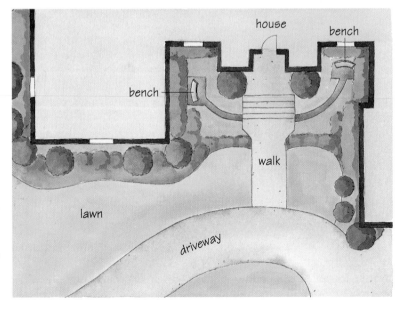

Sit Under Your Deck

If the only things enjoying the area underneath your deck are spiders, try this idea. Flat Rock, North Carolina, landscape architect Ed Lastein came up with a design that converts this space into a pleasant seating area.

Debris from above, inadequate shelter from rain, poor air circulation, and a messy dirt floor make sitting under a deck objectionable. Ed designed a cedar ceiling to solve the first three problems. Panels of inexpensive corrugated plastic—sandwiched between the floor of the deck and the new ceiling—catch leaves, dirt, and rainwater. To avoid cracks, Ed chose plastic rather than fiberglass panels.

The plastic is suspended below new 2 x 4 joists placed 16 inches apart. These joists are tapered so the valleys of the corrugations slope toward a gutter hung along one edge of the deck's fascia. It's important to slope the plastic enough to wash debris away, especially if you have a messy tree near the deck. The dropped ceiling will reduce vertical clearance under your deck, so make sure you have plenty of headroom. Also, keep in mind, the more complicated the shape of your deck, the higher the labor expense will be for a contractor to do the work.

No one wanted to sit under this deck before a ceiling and floor were added. Now, it's a favorite spot to relax.

Though the layered ceiling may not be totally drip proof, it offers enough protection to allow you to sit beneath your deck during a downpour. "But don't forget, it is an outdoor room, so rain can blow in from the sides," says Ed. "Furniture should be weather resistant."

Adding a ceiling fan is a good way to improve airflow. Before the finished ceiling is installed, drill a hole through the plastic at the peak of a corrugation. Drop the fan wire through the hole, and waterproof with silicone. Choose an exterior, flush-mount fan to add after the ceiling is in place. Not only is the breeze from the fan cooling, but it also helps keep bugs away.

The ceiling gives the under-deck area the finished appeal of a real room. So does the stone patio Ed added to take care of the dirt floor problem. You could also use brick, concrete, or pavers for a surface that is easy to sweep and cool underfoot.

After completing a project like this, you may find that you enjoy spending more time sitting under your deck than on it.

Jo Kellum

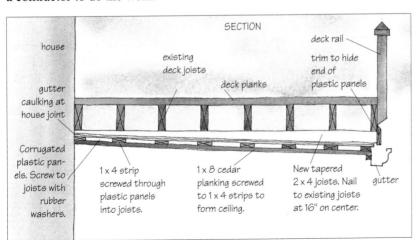

SECTION

house

gutter caulking at house joint

Corrugated plastic panels. Screw to joists with rubber washers.

existing deck joists

deck planks

1 x 4 strip screwed through plastic panels into joists.

1 x 8 cedar planking screwed to 1 x 4 strips to form ceiling.

deck rail

trim to hide end of plastic panels

New tapered 2 x 4 joists. Nail to existing joists at 16" on center.

gutter

Beautyberries clustered on woody stems rise out of billowy clouds of French hydrangea.

Branching Out

This fall, branch out of the cutting garden and into the woods. Make elegant arrangements with unconventional materials. Nature has plenty to offer, and its beauty can be displayed and enjoyed around your house.

Last fall I drove to a friend's farm and collected some treasures—fruit, seedpods, and limbs with brilliantly tinted foliage. Along the edge of fields I cut sagging branches from native persimmons and fruit-laden beautyberry. Wine-red pokeweed stems caught my eye. I also clipped small limbs of maple, sassafras, and sourwood. These native trees cover woodlots across the South with showy red, yellow, and orange foliage.

This is the season of change when autumn's splendor can be gathered and used to embellish your home.

Bucket loads of limbs sloshed around in water as I headed my truck toward home. Because most of the limbs were woody and sturdy, they didn't wilt during the drive.

Putting the arrangements together was simple. I tried to limit the amount of material used in each one, keeping them loose, uncluttered, and natural. The containers also had an earthy look.

I placed these touches of fall inside the house, by the front door, and on the deck. To preserve the seasonal look, I changed the water every few days to keep the arrangements fresh. Most of the combinations lasted much longer than cut flowers and had just as much impact.

BY CHARLIE THIGPEN / PHOTOGRAPHY JEAN ALLSOPP

Setting a few persimmons in a pot is simple and stunning. The skins on the fruit look sugarcoated, but don't take a bite until the fruit is deep orange and soft.

(Above) *Oakleaf hydrangea blooms are tawny brown, and the leaves provide outstanding fall color. Clusters of crabapples blush red and complement the hydrangea foliage.*

(Right) *Fiery foliage cut from maple and sassafras trees fills a bark-covered vase. Lotus seedpods collected from a pond have an almost alien look.*

PLANTS FOR A SHOWY FALL

Many of these colorful trees and shrubs can be planted in your yard. They will create a show in the landscape, and cuttings from these autumn favorites will add seasonal spice to the inside of your home. So get out your clippers and enjoy a little of the great outdoors, indoors.

Goldenrod (*Solidago* sp.) Native herbaceous perennial 3 to 5 feet tall with yellow, feathery blooms in late summer and early fall. This plant has gotten a bad rap as the source for hay fever, when ragweed, which emits pollen at the same time of year, is really the culprit. Many new, improved selections are available.

Beautyberry *(Callicarpa americana)* Native deciduous shrub 5 feet tall and wide. Rose-purple fruit August through November. Performs well in poor clay soils along woodland edges. Attracts wildlife and is ideal for naturalistic settings. Also comes in a white-berried selection called Lactea.

Oakleaf hydrangea *(Hydrangea quercifolia)* Deciduous shrub 6 feet tall and wide. Cone-shaped clusters of white flowers appear in spring and fade to brown by late summer. Large leaves can produce red-to-purple fall color. Older

Bloodred pokeweed stems create veiny lines for this arrangement, while yellow sprays of goldenrod arch out and add fullness.

stems have papery, exfoliating bark that curls off old wood. Great year-round plant for woodland settings.

Common persimmon *(Diospyros virginiana)* Small deciduous tree 35 feet tall with a spread of 20 feet. Produces edible fruit and has red-to-yellow fall color. Can be used in the landscape or around the vegetable garden, but should be planted in a location where falling fruit won't be a nuisance. Oriental persimmon *(D. kaki)* produces large fruit—twice the size of the common persimmon, yet doesn't grow as tall. It tops out at 25 feet.

Crabapple *(Malus angustifolia, M. floribunda)* Small deciduous tree 25 feet tall with a spread of 20 feet. Nice spring blooms ranging from pink to red depending on selection. Some produce large edible fruit. Crabapple is not a dependable tree for the Lower South. It is a relatively short-lived tree due to insect and disease problems. Like the persimmons, the fruit from crabapples can be a nuisance.

Sassafras *(Sassafras albidum)* Small deciduous tree 35 feet tall with a spread of 20 feet. Rarely seen in the landscape but often found in woodlands and along roadsides. Stunning fall color turning yellow, orange, and red. Three different leaf shapes can be found on the same tree. Tea is made from the roots, and the leaves produce an aromatic, lemony scent. ◇

(For sources see pages 250–251.)

A mixture of ground covers, succulents, grasses, roses, ferns, and shrubs (See pages 226-231.)

November

Moving the Garden

Whether you are moving plants across town or from one bed to another, here's how to ease the transition.

BY LINDA C. ASKEY
PHOTOGRAPHY VAN CHAPLIN

It isn't easy for a gardener to uproot. We plant so many memories and grow so many dreams. But sometimes we have to walk away and begin again.

That's where I found myself last fall—happy about a new home, but reluctant to leave my garden of nine years. I walked down the paths, thought of the friends who had shared their plants, and admired the outcome of seeds and cuttings I had reared into planthood. I just couldn't leave it all. I had to take some of it with me.

Fall is the best time to transplant, so I was fortunate. The plants I dug or divided had the entire winter to replace any roots that were injured or severed. They were ready to flourish in their new location by the time the weather warmed in spring.

Also, I had a couple of months before the house went up for sale. I dug up my treasures and replaced them with cool-season annuals before they could be missed by prospective buyers. To tell the truth, when I cleaned out the misplaced and overgrown plants, the garden had a stronger overall design. Just like the inside of the house when I cleaned out the closets and put away the clutter, the garden looked so much better that I wondered why I hadn't made these changes years ago.

TRIED-AND-TRUE TIPS

■ Set plants in containers at the same depth they were growing in the garden. Water them well, and continue to water periodically until they are planted in a new location.

■ Be sure that friends who help you dig your garden go home with plenty of divisions for their garden. A single clump of phlox can fall into four pieces when you dig it, and if several people have it growing, you know where to go if yours dies.

■ A speed of 45 m.p.h. seems to be the fastest I could drive without damaging plants in the bed of my truck.

■ If there are plants or furnishings you plan to take with you that are still in the garden when you are negotiating your contract, be sure to put it in writing that you are taking them.

■ Even if you are not moving, look at your garden as if you were. What would you change? Consider doing it so you can enjoy the results.

A piece of shade cloth is a better covering than a plastic or canvas tarp for plants in a truck. The porous material will not billow in the wind and blow off.

WHAT YOU'LL NEED

Potting soil—Depending on how many plants you are moving, you may need a lot of soil. Try to buy potting soil by the bale or make your own. I made mine from a pickup truck load of compost (from city leaf collections) mixed with soil conditioner I bought by the bag at the local garden center.

I couldn't leave behind the clustered bellflower (Campanula glomerata) *given to me by friend Nancy Goodwin.*

Pots and flats—Ask your gardening friends. Most of us can't bear to throw them away. Also, it's easy to pick up plenty wherever a landscape is being installed or by driving through the neighborhood on trash collection day.

Friends and neighbors—Getting started is the hardest part because it's difficult to dig up a garden you love. Besides, the task can seem overwhelming. Having the help of a friend to dig with you and move heavy plants can make the job a lot easier.

Labels—Just because you know what the plant is now doesn't mean you'll know when it's winter or when it is no longer in the context of your old garden. Label everything and write the information with an indelible marker.

Shade cloth—If you move plants in an open truck, buy a piece of shade cloth. Although nurseries use this material to shelter shade-loving plants from the hot sun, it makes a great tarp for your pickup. Plastic or canvas will billow and blow off. The open weave of shade cloth gives enough protection while letting some of the wind penetrate the covering. Expect to pay $1 to $1.75 per foot at a garden center. It's available in 6-foot widths. ◇

Harvesttime in the Flower Garden

Nothing could be happier in a Southern garden than a sweet potato, and flower gardeners have embraced the ornamental types that blanket the ground and trail from the edge of planters. Although perfectly adapted to thrive in our long, hot summer, Blackie, Marguarita, and Tricolor sweet potatoes face an uncertain future in fall.

So last autumn I dug mine up. Remembering that the edible forms of sweet potato are supposed to be harvested before frost, I troweled mine out of the big urn where it was in full cascade.

I let the foliage dry, and then placed it on the work bench in my basement through the winter. (It helps to put it somewhere you will see and remember it.) By spring, little shoots were appearing, letting me know it was time to plant it back in the garden.

Frost is not always fatal for the underground tubers. Sue Watkins at Tallahassee Nurseries tells me hers come back on

As winter threatens to put an end to the ornamental sweet potato, you can dig up the root and store it in a cool, dry place through the winter. Then in spring it will sprout again.

their own in Florida, even in areas where light freezes nip back the foliage. She says, "I replanted some barrels this spring, and there were these big potatoes that had overwintered and resprouted. We think it's perennial in mild winters, but not dangerously invasive." However, she recommends that gardeners in North Florida and similar climates of other states dig their tubers in fall. "It's like our caladiums," she explains. "They come back, but a percentage don't."

Be careful not to wound the tuber when you are digging it. Cuts and scrapes are an invitation to infection. If you accidentally nick one, dust it with sulfur to prevent rot.

When spring comes and the danger of frost has passed, consider planting the stored tubers in a pot. You can be sure they will get a good start that way, and they will be less likely to be food for the many creatures that are looking for a free lunch. *Linda C. Askey*

PHOTOGRAPHS: LINDA ASKEY, VAN CHAPLIN

Blackie sweet potato vine, like its chartreuse counterpart called Marguarita, has been a hit with gardeners this season. Many would like to have it again next year.

There is a perfect pansy for every sunny winter garden. (Left to right) Crystal Bowl, Crown, Maxim, and Majestic Giant selections are making their entrance into garden centers this month.

Pick a Pack of Pansies

Walk into almost any garden center this time of year and feast your eyes on a panorama of pansies. With so many flowers in every color and size imaginable, it's hard to decide.

Choose a pansy selection that is heat tolerant and cold hardy. Heat is a factor during fall planting time. Hot days and warm soil can make pansies spindly and weak. Followed with very cold weather, the flowers will flounder. A heat-tolerant selection will stay compact through warm autumn weather and take on winter in good condition.

Cold hardiness is especially important. Pansies thrive in cool weather. The true test comes when the mercury dips down into the low 20s. A good pansy selection is one that will bounce back with new blooms shortly after a blast of wintry weather. To help plants recover from frigid temperatures, keep them well fed. A dose of liquid plant food (15-30-15) every week will keep pansies well nourished. A light layer of pine straw also protects your plants from dehydrating winter winds.

PANSY PRIMER
Here's a guide to introduce you to four selections that are widely available.

Maxim brings back memories of old-fashioned gardens. It is a prolific provider of silver dollar-size flowers. These pansies have a "face," or dark blotch. Extremely heat tolerant and cold hardy, it's one of the best bets for flowers from autumn through winter and into spring. Many color choices are available.

Majestic Giant personifies the idea that bigger is better—pansies don't get any bigger than this. Majestic Giants are fragrant and grow on long stems that are perfect for picking. They are the mirror image of Maxim, with a major size adjustment. This selection does not begin its peak flower show until spring, blooming sporadically when the winter is cold. The plants remain healthy and strong but are uninspired to bloom. The very large flowers become top-heavy in a hard rain, with their blooms landing facedown in the garden.

Crystal Bowl sports blooms that are the same size as Maxim's and are equally heat tolerant and cold hardy. They bloom through thick and thin, and they bounce back from adverse weather conditions. The difference is in the flower. This selection has a clear color without a face. It is available in a rainbow of hues, with outstanding blue options.

Crown pansies are Crystal Bowl look-alikes on steroids. They are susceptible to heat and cold problems as are all large-flowered selections, but they leap into bloom in spring. The large flowers share Majestic Giant's weight problem when it rains. The flowers have a ruffle along the petal edge. There are not as many color options as Crystal Bowl, but they still have a good basic palette. *Ellen Riley*

AT A GLANCE

Light: minimum 4 hours direct sunlight
Fertilizer: Use time-release granular in fall and spring; liquid-feed weekly during winter.
Water: Keep moist in warm weather; water once a week, if dry, during winter. Water before a hard freeze.
Nice to Know: Pansies are perfect for picking. Make miniature bouquets regularly and new flowers will continue to form.

More Holly, By Golly!

It takes a lot of holly to deck your halls. Fortunately, there's an easy, inexpensive way to ensure your garden will always have plenty: Root some cuttings. It's simple, and November is a good time to try.

Step 1: Assemble the supplies you'll need—a few small containers, a saucer, water, a knife, pruners, a clear plastic jug, and some holly cuttings. The cuttings should be 4 to 6 inches long. Just about any kind of holly will do.

Step 2: Strip the lowest one or two sets of leaves from a cutting. Now use a sharp knife to slice away bark from two opposite sides of the bottom of the cutting, starting about a half-inch from the bottom. When you finish, the bottom should be pointed and wedge shaped. This exposes more of the rooting surface to the soil.

Step 3: Pour a little rooting powder (available at most garden centers) into a saucer. Dip the cut end into water to moisten it; then dip it into the rooting powder. Gently tap the cutting to shake off any excess powder. Discard all unused powder remaining in the saucer. Returning it to its original container could possibly spread disease to future cuttings.

Step 4: Fill a small pot with moist potting soil. Press a pencil point into the center of the soil to make a hole. Insert the cutting into the hole and firm soil around it. Cut the bottom out of a clear, plastic jug. (A 2-liter soda bottle works well.) Place the jug over the potted cutting. It will act as a greenhouse, keeping in humidity, speeding the rooting process.

Step 5: Voilà! If you keep the soil moist and put the cutting near a bright window (no hot sun), roots should form in four to eight weeks. In the Coastal and Tropical South, plant the rooted cutting outside. Elsewhere, place the cutting in a cold frame for the first winter. Or grow the cutting indoors this winter and transplant it to the garden next spring. *Steve Bender*

PHOTOGRAPHS: JEAN ALLSOPP

DOUBLE YOUR PLEASURE

For a special touch in easy flower arrangements, look to your houseplants.

Put a peacock and a sparrow side by side and the difference in colorful feathers is obvious. You can make the same comparison with houseplants. Rex begonia, calathea, and prayer plant all produce showy leaves that are anything but plain-Jane green. Use the plants as decorative accents, and double your enjoyment by taking a few cuttings for your next arrangement.

Rex begonia *(Begonia* x *rex-cultorum)* leaves complement a multitude of flowers. Choose from selections with foliage ranging from silver and pink to ruby red, or try the green selections with variegated, somewhat hairy leaves. Rex begonia's stems are not rigid, so use them in small arrangements where a few stems in water will do. Cut stems short so the leaves hug the container. Snuggle flowers around them to make a full display. In large arrangements, cut the stems a bit longer, allowing the leaves to droop gracefully over the edge of the container. Expect cut Rex begonia leaves to last three or four days.

Prayer plant *(Maranta leuconeura massangeana)* has brilliant red-ribbed foliage with lime-green splotches down

Two Rex begonia leaves, one stem of pink stock, and a few sprigs of heather turn a chair-back container into a tiny, elegant arrangement.

BY ELLEN RILEY
PHOTOGRAPHY TINA CORNETT

A mint julep cup is the perfect host for silver-and-pink Rex begonia leaves, lavender freesia, and heather. The flowers, foliage, and container all have cool silver tones.

the center. These leaves look stunning with warm-colored flowers such as red freesia, sunflowers, and small mums. Each leaf has a very short stem, but longer stem branches bearing several leaves can be cut from a mature plant. The cuttings remain fresh in water for up to a week. Prayer plant closes its leaves at night, so an arrangement may change in appearance from day to evening.

Calathea foliage resembles prayer plant, but there are significant differences. Many calatheas have foliage with deep burgundy undersides. This adds as much color and interest to an arrangement as the lovely pattern on the front. Calatheas have rigid stems that remain upright and may be used with florist foam. They will stay fresh for up to one week. Peacock plant *(Calathea makoyana)* sports intricately patterned leaves in shades of green. Sander-ana calathea (*C. ornata* Sanderana) boasts leaves with a deep green background and salmon-pink stripes.

Enjoy the beauty these plants will bring to your home. Then double your pleasure by including their leaves in an arrangement. You'll be proud as a peacock. ◇

Leaves of calathea, prayer plant, and Rex begonia and a few flowers are all that's needed to set a casual table for company.

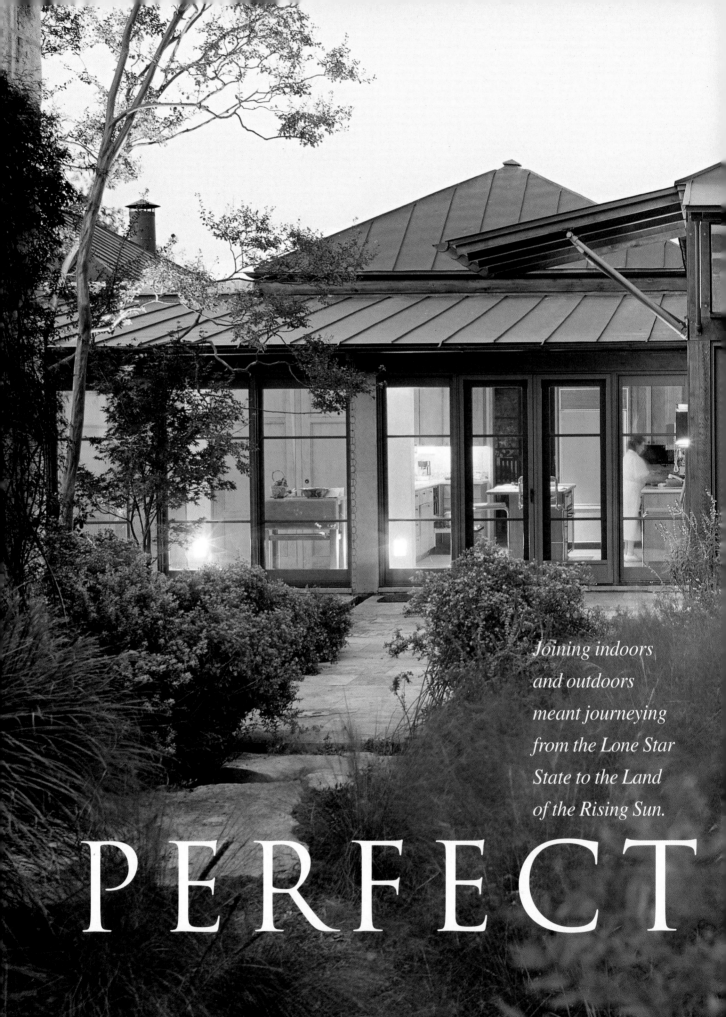

Joining indoors and outdoors meant journeying from the Lone Star State to the Land of the Rising Sun.

PERFECT

UNION

BY STEVE BENDER / PHOTOGRAPHY VAN CHAPLIN

"In Japan, the landscape reflects nature. So we thought if you're going to do a Texas/Japanese-style house, you should also do a naturalistic landscape."

Landscape architect Rosa Finsley

Lit by the setting sun, the rosy pink plumes of Gulf muhly grass blaze away in the North Texas autumn.

Garland and Mollie Lasater wanted to build a house in Fort Worth that was totally Texas. So they did the logical thing. They gathered their architect, Ted Flato of San Antonio, and flew off to visit Japan.

The result is a remarkable design that blends Texas limestone foundations and cedar framing with flared copper roofs reminiscent of pagodas. To the first-time visitor, this is pretty wild stuff. But it all works, due to exterior walls made mostly of glass that blur the distinction between indoors and outside. Stand in any room and you feel immersed in pure North Texas habitat. The complete integration of the house and land reflects valuable lessons learned in Japan.

Such unity was their goal, says Garland, not simply an Oriental look. "We didn't want to build a Japanese house in Fort Worth or a French house or anything else," he explains. "We wanted a house where the indoors and outdoors flowed together, so when you went there, you'd say,

'By gosh, this is a house that belongs right here.'"

The gardens, designed by landscape architect Rosa Finsley of Kings Creek Gardens in Cedar Hill, Texas, are just as extraordinary. Her designs typically feature ornamental grasses, perennials, and shrubs adapted to the unforgiving Texas climate and soil. She continues that tradition here with complex blends of colors, textures, flowers, and foliage that mirror an indigenous community of hardy plants.

(Top) *Aromatic asters, ornamental grasses, and a slew of salvias defy the harsh climate and rocky soil to fill fall with flowers.* **(Left)** *Stacked native limestone draped with shrubs and perennials magnifies the sound of water pouring from a spillway near the back of the house.* **(Above)** *In the front, water wells up from a hole bored through a native stone and trickles over the sides.*

Every garden needs a seating area. Here an arbor covered with crossvine shades a limestone terrace. Compacted, decomposed granite gives the adjacent courtyard a natural look.

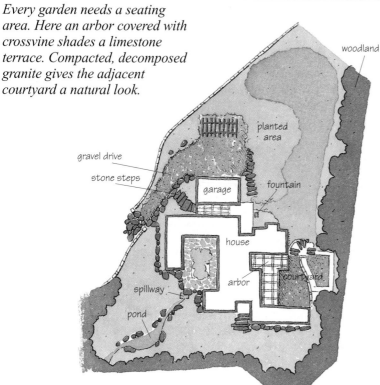

woodland

planted area

gravel drive

stone steps

garage

fountain

house

spillway

arbor

courtyard

pond

"In Japan, the landscape reflects nature," Rosa observes. "So we thought if you're going to do a Texas/Japanese-style house, you should also do a naturalistic landscape."

Autumn, often overlooked elsewhere in the area, is beautiful here. Paths wind past sweeps of aromatic aster *(Aster oblongifolius)* and a menagerie of flowering salvias. Graceful plumes of maiden grass *(Miscanthus sinensis* Gracillimus), Lindheimer's muhly grass *(Muhlenbergia lindheimeri)*, and ravenna grass *(Erianthus ravennae)* punctuate the air. In late afternoon, the pink sprays of Gulf muhly grass *(M. filipes)*, lit by the setting sun, positively glow.

"What we enjoy most about it is finding new views and new ways of looking at it. Actually, we designed that into it, so as you turn a corner or sit in a different location, you see a different view."

Garland Lasater

(**Above**) *Grasses and perennials mirror the look of the original prairie and provide a haven for native bees, birds, and wildlife.* (**Right**) *This complex mixture of hardy ground covers, succulents, grasses, roses, ferns, and shrubs greets visitors on their way to the front door.*

Mollie looks forward to the extended progression of color that stamps every season with its own identity. "You're almost in tears because one plant is fading out," she says. "But before you know it, something new is coming in."

As lovely as the plants are, says Rosa, they serve a broader purpose than beauty. "We're basically a prairie here with woodlands along the drainage areas," she observes. "So the grasses and perennials were here originally. Using them is good aesthetically, but also environmentally. It means that the bees, butterflies, and birds that evolved with these plants can live here with us. We can coexist and be good company."

Though modest in size, the garden feels larger, thanks to pockets of plants you can't see at once. "What we enjoy most about it is finding new views and new ways of looking at it," comments Garland. "Actually, we designed that into it, so as you turn a corner or sit in a different location, you see a different view. That element of surprise has been really delightful."

So delightful, in fact, that visitors immediately sense the special nature of the place. "The first thing people say is, 'This is such a retreat—how do you ever leave?'" notes Mollie. "And I begin to feel like that. More and more, I treasure the days I don't have to go anywhere." ◇

Mailbox arrangement with apples, citrus, berries, evergreens, and pinecones (See pages 242–243.)

December

Beribboned sunflower seedhead wreaths and Miracle Meal pinecones glued to sticks decorate this bird lover's winter window box.

HOLIDAY TREATS
For Songbirds

Winter birds flock to specially selected goodies.

If you love the idea of a winter garden full of feathered friends, combine outdoor decorating with backyard bird feeding. Simple techniques in a festive setting bring overwintering birds flying in to chow down every morning and afternoon. Choose any weatherproof ribbons that please your eye; the birds won't care. They *will,* however, notice the menu.

Start with a shopping list of the foods that birds love. Each species has its preferences. Proso millet, the tiny white seeds in bird-food mixes that are rejected and scattered on the ground by other birds, is the preferred food of ground-feeding birds such as doves, juncos, and towhees. Niger (thistle) seeds

(From left) *Black oil sunflower seeds, proso millet, and niger (thistle) seeds attract many friends from cardinals to doves to goldfinches.*

are favored by goldfinches and pine siskins who cling to feed; small black oil sunflower seeds bring in a whole host of birds, including cardinals, grosbeaks, woodpeckers, titmice, and chickadees. All species love the high-fat, high-protein peanut butter treat called Miracle Meal (see recipe on page 238). Even insect eaters such as bluebirds and Carolina wrens that may not visit a seed-feeding station show up for this treat.

When the birds arrive, the fun really begins. Every species has characteristic behaviors that folks who feed birds get to see up close and personal. LuAnn Craighton, the manager of Conservation Studies at Callaway Gardens in Pine Mountain, Georgia, has introduced

BY LUCINDA MAYS / PHOTOGRAPHY VAN CHAPLIN

HOLIDAY TREATS FOR THE BIRDS

LuAnn Craighton of Callaway Gardens passes along the recipes that keep her birds happy.

BASIC MIRACLE MEAL

2 cups smooth or chunky peanut butter
2 cups shortening
2 cups flour
6 to 8 cups cornmeal

Melt peanut butter and shortening in a large saucepan over medium heat; stir in dry ingredients. Turn dough out into a wax paper-lined 13- x 9-inch pan. Let stand until cool enough to stiffen. Cut into rectangles that fit standard suet feeders. Store extras in the refrigerator.

Miracle Meal Cookies: Make a batch of Basic Miracle Meal. While mixture is still warm, flatten it by hand to ½-inch thickness. Cut into shapes, and allow to cool. The scraps can be kneaded and reflattened while still warm.

Popcorn Strings: String unsalted popcorn onto strong thread using a short needle.

Garlands: Thread plain toasted oat O-shaped cereal onto inexpensive, stiff ribbon.

Goodie Baskets: Oven-dry tangerine rind halves until stiff. Punch three evenly spaced holes near the cut edge of rinds. Attach 8-inch-long narrow satin ribbons as hangers. Fill with raisins and sunflower seeds.

Sticks and Cones: Hot-glue pinecones onto 18-inch-long dowels. Use a pastry bag to pipe warm Basic Miracle Meal between the "petals" of the cones. Add extra melted shortening if meal is too stiff to pipe.

Sunflower Wreaths: Work from the back of a dried sunflower seedhead; cut a small circle from the center of head. Pass a 24-inch ribbon through the hole, and tie it at the top in a bow with generous streamers.

hundreds of people to backyard bird attracting. A real veteran of observing birds, LuAnn suggests placing your holiday treats outside convenient windows so you can start your winter mornings with coffee and the first avian antics of the day.

Chickadees and titmice are curious and nimble; they'll hang upside down to check out new things. And they'll take a seed, fly away to eat it, and come back for more. Cardinals, purple finches, and house finches will gobble until they've had their fill. Evening grosbeaks are the biggest feasters of all. It takes a disturbance to chase them off, which is just what happens when a raucous blue jay blows in. Juncos tend to dine in groups. If you see one junco, keep looking; there are more nearby.

Some birds, such as doves, are very nervous. It's easier to watch them from behind window blinds or sheer curtains. No high-tech equipment is needed to enjoy the spectacle, but it is nice to have a pair of binoculars and a good field guide to identify an unusual visitor that flutters in.

Who benefits more from setting out a buffet for the birds—the watcher or the watched? Certainly, birds gain from extra food supplies in late winter and early spring. And our days are enhanced by the sprightly activity in our frosty gardens. That's worth a spoonful of peanut butter and some seeds.

(For sources see pages 250–251.)

(Above) *Gifts for bird lovers include feeders of all sorts, the classic Peterson's field guide, a birdwatcher's journal to log in each new bird, and a pair of binoculars.*

(Top) *Miracle Meal Cookies (see recipe at left) and scattered raisins attract birds that might not usually visit feeders.*

Bundle Up Your Pots

Help shield your container plants from freezing temperatures with a stylish winter coat.

It's winter, and blustery breezes send us scurrying for coats, hats, and mufflers. Your plants need coats as well. The north wind is busy wrapping frigid fingers around planted containers on patios and porches. A container will freeze quicker than the ground, so a plant in a pot needs insulation. Bundle it up in an easy-to-make overcoat that will diminish the damage winter winds can cause a containerized tree or shrub. And while you're at it, decorate for holiday fun.

Step 1: Wrap the container with two layers of plastic bubble wrap. Fasten these with heavy-duty plastic tape. Fold the excess underneath the container.

Step 2: Cover the bubble wrap with burlap, overlapping the fabric's edges. Wrap plastic-coated wire around the pot to secure the burlap.

Step 3: Add holiday decorations, such as a bow, magnolia leaves, pinecones, etc., to the container, if desired. Nandina berries can be added to the plant if appropriate. After the holidays, replace the colored burlap with natural-colored fabric, and wrap with rope to fasten.

CONTAINER SURVIVAL GUIDE

When the temperature drops into the low twenties, a few extra precautions help container plants cope.

■ Water plants thoroughly. Freezing temperatures dehydrate soil and roots.

■ Use a large plastic bag to cover the plant and container at night. Tuck the bag's edges underneath the pot to prevent cold air from drifting up into the bag. Remember: The bag must be removed before the sun hits it in the morning. In extremely cold weather, foliage might burn where the plastic and the leaves come in contact.

■ Terra-cotta is susceptible to freeze damage. Bring special containers into a garage or heated shed for winter.

Ellen Riley

MATERIALS

PLASTIC BUBBLE WRAP

HEAVY-DUTY PLASTIC TAPE

BURLAP—PLAIN OR HOLIDAY COLOR

PLASTIC-COATED WIRE

ROPE OR HOLIDAY RIBBON

BOW, MAGNOLIA LEAVES, PINECONES, OR OTHER ORNAMENTS (OPTIONAL)

A ligustrum topiary is wrapped up for holiday celebrations and insulation. Nandina berries, added to the foliage, act as ornaments. After the holidays, use plain burlap and rope to blend containers into the landscape.

Terra-cotta
TRANSFORMATION

With a little imagination, you can turn ordinary containers into original handcrafted pots that complement your home's decor.

BY CHARLIE THIGPEN
PHOTOGRAPHY JEAN ALLSOPP

If you're like most gardeners, you already have a stack of terra-cotta pots around back. Grab a few and dress them up using one of these techniques. It won't cost much, and you'll have a new container that can become a nice decorative element with the right houseplant.

Strips of exfoliating oakleaf hydrangea bark make the containers at left look like small tree trunks. Use a glue gun to apply glue directly to a clean pot. Then press strips of hydrangea bark onto the glue. Overlap strips until they completely cover the container. These brown papery pieces of bark are relatively sturdy and hold up well if not roughly handled. The pots shown here were made two years ago and still look great.

Moss and branches camouflage the pot shown in the inset photo at left. Attach several winged sweet gum branches to thin-gauge wire, and wrap them around a pot. Push Spanish moss down into the exposed wire to cover it and help maintain an earthy, loose look. Wedge dried mushrooms between the wires so they look as though they're growing out of the mossy background.

1 We used silicone to attach pea gravel to this pot shown at right. Terra-cotta is fired clay which is very porous, so hot glue and silicone will readily adhere to it. This pea gravel pot was easy to make, but it did take time because individual pebbles were pressed onto the pot one by one.

To make a pebble pot, first prep the surface using sandpaper to rough up the container and remove any loose debris. Then wipe it clean, removing any dust with a dry cloth. Apply a small dab of silicone adhesive to the pot, but don't use

(Left) Terra-cotta pots clothed in bark achieve an earthy look. (Inset) Moss, branches, and dried mushrooms lend a dramatic flair to this pot.

too much at once because you want it to be tacky as you place the stone. Next, press pea gravel into the silicone until it bonds to the pot.

Keep a damp rag handy because the process can get a little messy. Cover the pot completely until none of its original surface is exposed. Let the silicone dry; then slip the plant you select into the container and top with gravel.

2 You can make a ceramic-tile container using this same technique. First, break a few tiles into small pieces. To do this, simply wrap the tiles in a thick cloth and tap with a hammer. The cloth will protect you from any flying debris. The broken pieces can be sharp so you may want to wear gloves.

Because the pot's exterior is curved, small pieces of tile work better. Clean the pot well, using the same method as for the pebble pot, before you attach the tile. Apply a small amount of silicone, making sure the tile has enough adhesive to completely cover the back. Leave enough space between each piece of tile so you can later work grout into the joints.

Once the silicone has dried, mix up a batch of grout to the consistency of thick mud. Work grout into the seams, filling them completely. Don't worry about getting grout on the tiles. As it begins to dry, you can wipe it off with a damp rag.

3 The pink painted pot has a stucco-like texture. If you like this finish, simply grab a paintbrush and apply a thick coat of exterior latex paint. While the paint is still wet, sprinkle crushed gravel or coarse sand on the pot. This gives it a bumpy-textured surface.

These creative containers were made for indoor use. Plants should be left in their plastic nursery pots and simply slipped into the new containers. You can pull the plants out of the containers and water them outside or in the sink. ◇

Merry MAILBOX

BY ELLEN RILEY / PHOTOGRAPHY VAN CHAPLIN

Begin your holiday decorating at one of the most visible points in your yard—the mailbox. Holly, magnolia, boxwood, and other evergreens are the provisions you'll need to begin. Then, add more color and presence with nandina berries and pinecones. A grand bow of crimson ribbon is the crowning touch to welcome all who pass by.

Florist foam is the starting point for this project. Adapt the forms to fit any size or shape mailbox. If the mailbox is small or the decoration understated, cut the foam in half before you begin. If built into a pillar, use full-size forms on top of the column. The secret to savvy decorations is scale.

Step 1: Completely cover one florist foam block with green sheet moss. Wrap a piece of chicken wire around it, with long edges extending several inches beyond the form. Secure the long edge of the chicken wire to itself with plastic-coated wire. At each end, bend the chicken wire over on itself to enclose the moss and florist foam. It should resemble a moss- and wire-covered brick. Repeat with the other block of foam.

Step 2: Soak bricks in water until the florist foam is thoroughly moist.

Step 3: Use plastic-coated wire to fasten the two blocks together at each of the long ends, leaving a loop of wire between them. Straddle the blocks on each side of the mailbox, like saddlebags, with the wire loop going over the top. Adjust the length of the wires to secure each block in the middle of the mailbox sides.

Step 4: Attach the outdoor bow to the top of the mailbox, wiring it to the back wire loop. Insert greenery into the florist foam, cutting stems short. Work from side to side, filling each block with assorted greenery until the forms are no longer visible. *Tip:* Do not arrange one side and then the other. The forms will slide off the mailbox with unequal weight.

Step 5: Attach pinecones to florist picks using extra wire to secure. Wire nandina berry stems to picks. Push the picks into the foam.

Step 6: To keep the arrangement fresh, pour a pitcher of water gently over the florist foam every few days. ◇

TOOLS & MATERIALS

2 BLOCKS FLORIST FOAM

GREEN SHEET MOSS

CHICKEN WIRE

PLASTIC-COATED WIRE

WIRE CUTTERS

I LARGE BOW MADE FROM OUTDOOR RIBBON

GREENERY, PINECONES, AND BERRIES

4-INCH FLORIST PICKS

(Left) *A festive mailbox is the first glimpse of a holiday welcome. Evergreens, berries, and pinecones will last through the season.*

(Top, left) *Apples and citrus, attached with florist picks, add a handsome look to a large mailbox arrangement.*

RED CEDAR

The True Survivor

Dogged, rugged, and supremely adaptable, this native evergreen gives Southerners hope for the future.

If any tree could claim eternity, that tree would be red cedar. Stoic as a monk, steady as the moon, it plants itself across our land in a seeming demonstration of life's unconquerable spirit. Finding sustenance in the most meager of soils, it grows calmly, faithfully, and always.

Red cedar *(Juniperus virginiana)* isn't a true cedar at all, but a native juniper. In most places, it's spirelike and conical, growing 40 to 50 feet tall, slowly spreading near the top with age. Its shape makes the tree an excellent windbreak. Many a rural Southerner employs cedars to line country lanes and shelter farmhouses and fields.

But farmers aren't responsible for most cedars. That honor goes to the

BY STEVE BENDER
PHOTOGRAPHY VAN CHAPLIN

birds. Each fall and winter, clusters of berries weigh down the conifer's limber branches like bunches of tiny grapes—that is, until the birds arrive. Robins, cedar waxwings, mockingbirds, cardinals, and brown thrashers gobble the frosty blue fruit; then they distribute seeds wherever they perch. This explains the inevitable cedars growing beside fences and under telephone wires.

While red cedar thrives in any well-drained soil, its affinity for alkaline ground makes it a natural marker for buried deposits of limestone. Indeed, just about anywhere cedars dot the landscape, from the hills of Tennessee to Southwestern prairies, the chalky remnants of a prehistoric sea lie close beneath the surface.

Despite its dignity and utter tenacity, the red cedar's story in the South is largely one of human

Stately and dignified, red cedars lend welcome color to this quiet country road in winter.

exploitation. Few trees produce as fragrant, beautiful, rot-resistant, and useful a wood. The wood makes superb, long-lasting fence posts, flooring, siding, and outdoor furniture. (Western red cedar *[Thuja plicata]* quickly rots with ground contact and is not a good substitute.) Cedar

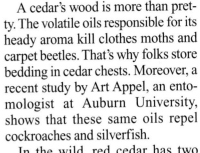

log houses last practically forever.

The soft wood is also easy to work. In the Tidewater village of Tunis Mills, Maryland, Nick Mielke finds cedars that have been blown down in storms, and he carves their wood into waterfowl decoys he sells on the Internet. Rather than painting the wood, Nick takes advantage of its natural colors. For example, the dark neck of a canvasback decoy comes from the cedar's red heartwood. The creamy-white sapwood forms the duck's wings.

Clusters of attractive blue berries are heavy enough to weigh down the branches of some cedars in fall and winter. But hungry birds soon relieve the trees of their burden.

PHOTOGRAPH: ALLEN ROKACH

A cedar's wood is more than pretty. The volatile oils responsible for its heady aroma kill clothes moths and carpet beetles. That's why folks store bedding in cedar chests. Moreover, a recent study by Art Appel, an entomologist at Auburn University, shows that these same oils repel cockroaches and silverfish.

In the wild, red cedar has two natural enemies—fire and ice. Ice storms can split trees right down the middle, even though most will survive. But wildfire kills cedars. Ironically, it's the absence of fire that has allowed red cedar to invade grasslands in Oklahoma and Texas, much to the ire and consternation of ranchers.

"Red cedar is a great survivor," says Bill Ross, Extension forestry specialist in Stillwater, Oklahoma. "It's one of those species that does really well in the presence of human beings. The tree's encroachment is largely a result of our removing wildfire from the ecosystem." The Oklahoma Red Cedar Association encourages landowners to harvest red cedars, not burn them, and eventually turn the tree into a managed, renewable resource.

It's that dogged survivability and a sense of continuity that make red cedar special to so many people. Venerable, old red cedars grace more cemeteries and historic estates than perhaps any other tree. And each December, Southerners venture out into fields to cut a new cedar Christmas tree, confident that there will always be more.

A red cedar symbolizes hope for the future. Figuratively and literally, it is evergreen.

There are numerous forms of red cedar recommended for garden use. For sources see pages 250–251. ◇

Rugged and resourceful, red cedars make superb windbreaks. Large numbers such as these near Greenwood, South Carolina, usually indicate limestone deposits under the soil.

January

WINTER SCENTS
Pages 12–13: **Witch hazel, Wintersweet, Winter daphne, Winter honeysuckle, Star magnolia, and Japanese flowering apricot** available from Woodlanders, Inc., Greer Gardens. **Paperwhites** available from K. Van Bourgondien & Sons, Inc., The Daffodil Mart.

THE WELL-PLACED CAMELLIA
Pages 18–19: **Camellias** available from Camellia Forest Nursery, Nuccio's Nurseries.

A PERSONAL APPEAL FROM LENTEN ROSE
Pages 20–21: **Lenten rose** available from André Viette Farm and Nursery, Wayside Gardens.

February

TOMATO MAN
Pages 30–32: **Tomato seed** available from W. Atlee Burpee & Company, Tomato Growers Supply Company, Gardener's Supply Company **(garden supplies)**, Gardens Alive.

March

PARADE OF LETTUCE
Pages 48–50: **Lettuce seeds** available from Shepherd's Garden Seeds, The Cook's Garden, Johnny's Selected Seeds.

DON'T PLANT GRASS WHERE GRASS WON'T GROW
Pages 54–55: **Asian star jasmine** available from Logee's Greenhouses, Louisiana Nursery, Woodlanders, Inc. **Wedelia** available from nurseries in tropical areas.

THERE'S NOTHING WRONG WITH A LITTLE PRIVACY
Pages 60–61: **Loquat** available from Ron's Rare Plants & Seeds, Louisiana Nursery. **Lusterleaf holly** available from Forestfarm. **Southern red cedar** available from Forestfarm, Woodlanders, Inc. **Japanese anise** available from Logee's Greenhouses, Louisiana Nursery, Woodlanders, Inc. **Oleander** available from Louisiana Nursery, Logee's Greenhouses. **Osmanthus** available from Louisiana Nursery, Heronswood Nursery Ltd.

CLUELESS IN THE FLOWERBED
Pages 62–63: **Maiden grass** available from Louisiana Nursery, Wayside Gardens. **Rough heliopsis** available from Wildflowers from Nature's Way. **Eared coreopsis** available from Louisiana Nursery, Owen Farms, André Viette Farm and Nursery.

EVERYTHING'S COMING UP ROSES
Page 66: **Roses** available from Antique Rose Emporium, Heirloom Old Garden Roses, Vintage Gardens, Petals from the Past.

April

EDITORS' NOTEBOOK
Page 74: *The Southern Living Garden Book* available by calling (800) 884-3935.

HIGH STAKES
Pages 76–79: **Marguarita sweet potato vine** available from Lakeview Gardens.

FOREVER YOUNG
Pages 86–89: **Louisiana iris** available from Louisiana Nursery, Bois D'Arc Gardens. **Bearded iris** available from André Viette Farm and Nursery, Wayside Gardens.

BLOSSOMS OF THE HEART
Pages 90–93: **Dogwoods** available from Fairweather Gardens, Forestfarm, Greer Gardens.

May

A GARDEN WINNER
Page 101: **Corydalis** available from White Flower Farm.

BASIL BASICS
Page 105: **Basil seeds** available from The Cook's Garden, Shepherd's Garden Seeds. **Basil plants** available from W. Atlee Burpee & Company.

FRINGE BENEFITS JUST IN TIME
Page 106: **Chinese fringe tree** available from Woodlanders, Forestfarm, Fairweather Gardens.

THIS ROSE IS FOR REAL
Page 108: **Pink Flower Carpet Rose,** call 1-800-580-5930 for the name of the nearest Flower Carpet retailer.

June

ANNABELLE SHINES IN SUMMER SHADE
Page 127: **Annabelle hydrangea** available from Louisiana Nursery, Niche Gardens, Wayside Gardens, Woodlanders, Inc.

CELOSIA WORTH A SECOND LOOK
Page 128: **Wheat celosia** available from Park Seed.

HIGH-VALUE VEGETABLES
Page 133: **Vegetable seeds** available from Shepherd's Garden Seeds, The Cook's Garden, W. Atlee Burpee & Co., Park Seed.

ALL IN LINE
Pages 134–136: **Adirondack chairs** available from Art Campbell, Sa Gairdin.

ALMOST HEAVEN
Pages 140–145: **Easter lily** available from Dutch Gardens. **Orientals and Asiatics** available from K. Van Bourgondien & Sons, Inc., The Daffodil Mart. **Tiger lilies** available from K. Van Bourgondien & Sons, Inc., Dutch Gardens. **Formosa lilies** available from Wayside Gardens and Plant Delights Nursery. **Regal lilies** are available from Wayside Gardens and K. Van Bourgondien & Sons, Inc., **Madonna lilies** are available from Carroll Gardens. **Lilies** are available from B&D Lilies.

July

SUMMER'S JEWEL
Pages 150–152: **Butterfly bush** available from Forestfarm, Greene Hill Nursery, Louisiana Nursery.

PRACTICALLY PERFECT PLANTS
Page 153: **Firecracker plant** available from Louisiana Nursery. **Coral plant** available from Logee's Greenhouses.

DRESSING A SHADED BED
Page 155: **Italian arum** available from Goodness Grows.

A PLACE IN THE SHADE
Page 156: For more information on **Stabilizer,** call Stabilizer Solutions, Inc.

August

CARNIVAL OF COLOR
Pages 166–168: **Zinnias** available from W. Atlee Burpee & Co., Shepherd's Garden Seeds, Johnny's Selected Seeds, Park Seed.

WHITER SHADE OF PALE
Page 169: **Variegated miscanthus** available from Twombly Nursery, Louisiana Nursery, Plant Delights Nursery. **Glacier English ivy** available from Logee's Greenhouses, Carroll Gardens, Plant Delights Nursery. **Snow-on-the-mountain** available from Ron's Rare Plants & Seeds, Johnny's Selected Seeds.

A COURTYARD CONVERSION
Page 173: **Concrete stain** available from L.M. Scofield Company.

October

THIS LILY DESERVES A LOOK
Page 207: **Eucharis (Amazon) lily** bulbs available for shipment in March from Mellinger's, Inc.

BRANCHING OUT

Pages 210–213: **Beautyberry** *(Callicarpa americana)* available from Woodlanders, Inc., Niche Gardens, We-Du Nurseries. **Persimmon** *(Diospyrus virginiana)* available from Forestfarm, Louisiana Nursery, Woodlanders, Inc. **Crabapple** *(Malus angustifolia)* available from Louisiana Nursery, Woodlanders, Inc. **Crabapple** *(Malus floribunda)* available from Forestfarm. **Sassafras** available from Forestfarm, Louisiana Nursery, Woodlanders, Inc.

December

HOLIDAY TREATS FOR SONGBIRDS

Pages 236-238: **Books, binoculars, feeders, and other accessories** available from Duncraft.

RED CEDAR: THE TRUE SURVIVOR

Pages 244-247: **Red cedar** *(Juniperus viriniana),* **Lawrenceville** selection available from Woodlanders, Inc. **Pendula, Sky Rocket, and Spartan** available from Girard. **Grey Owl, Royo, Sky Rocket, and Sparkling Sky Rocket** available from Roslyn Nursery.

SOURCES

André Viette Farm and Nursery (O), (800) 492-2294, no minimum order, catalog $6.

Antique Rose Emporium (O), (800) 441-0002, no minimum order, catalog $5.

Art Campbell, Sa Gairdin (R), 222 Zion Church Road, Easley, SC 29642, (864) 850-1138.

B&D Lilies (O), (360) 385-1738, $20 minimum order, catalog $3.

Bois D'Arc Gardens (O), (504) 446-2329, $25 minimum order, catalog $2.

Camellia Forest Nursery (O), 125 Carolina Forest Road, Chapel Hill, NC 27516, catalog $2.

Carroll Gardens (O), (800) 638-6334, no minimum order, catalog free.

The Cook's Garden (O), (800) 457-9703, no minimum order, catalog free.

The Daffodil Mart (O), (800) 255-2852, $50 minimum order, catalog free.

Duncraft (O), for customer service call (800) 763-7878.

Dutch Gardens (O), (800) 818-3861, no minimum order, catalog free.

Fairweather Gardens (O), (609) 451-6261, no minimum order, catalog $3.

Forestfarm (O), 99 Tetherow Rd., Williams, OR 97544, (541) 846-7629, no minimum order, catalog $4.

Gardens Alive (O), (Neem), (812) 537-8650, catalog available.

Gardener's Supply Company (O), (garden supplies), (800) 955-3370, no minimum order, catalog free.

Girard (O), (440) 466-2881, $20 minimum order, catalog free.

Goodness Grows (O), (706) 743-5055, (available in fall only) $20 minimum order, catalog free.

Greene Hill Nursery (R), 5027 Hwy. 147, Waverly, AL 36879, (334) 864-7500.

Greer Gardens (O), (800) 548-0111, no minimum order, catalog $3.

Heirloom Old Garden Roses (O), (503) 538-1576, no minimum order, catalog $5.

Heronswood Nursery Ltd. (O), (360) 297-4172, $5 minimum shipping cost, catalog $5 for a 2-year subscription.

Johnny's Selected Seeds (O), (207) 437-4301, no minimum order, catalog free.

K. Van Bourgondien & Sons, Inc. (O), (800) 622-9997, no minimum order, catalog free.

L.M. Scofield Company (R), To place an order, or to receive information, call (800) 800-9900.

Lakeview Gardens (O), (704) 456-6845, minimum order three flats, catalog not available.

Logee's Greenhouses (O), (860) 774-8038, $20 minimum order, catalog free.

Louisiana Nursery (O), (318) 948-3696, $50 minimum order, catalog $6.

Mellinger's, Inc. (O), (800) 321-7444, no minimum order, catalog free.

Niche Gardens (O), 111 Dawson Rd., Chapel Hill, SC 27516, (919) 967-0078, (minimum order $35) catalog $3.

Nuccio's Nurseries (O), (818) 794-3383.

Owen Farms (O), (901) 635-1588, $5 minimum shipping cost, catalog $2.

Park Seed (O), (864) 223-7333, no minimum order, catalog free.

Petals from the Past (O), 16034 County Road 29, Jemison, AL 35805.

Plant Delights Nursery (O), (919) 772-4794, $25 minimum order, catalog for 10 stamps or a box of chocolates.

Ron's Rare Plants & Seeds (O), (708) 862-1993, no minimum order, no catalog.

Roslyn Nursery (O), (516) 643-9347, no minimum order, catalog $3.

Shepherd's Garden Seeds (O), (860) 482-3638, no minimum order, catalog free.

Stabilizer Solutions, Inc. (M), (800) 336-2468.

The Southern Living Garden Book (O), (800) 884-3935, $29.95 softbound, $34.95 hardbound.

Tomato Growers Supply Company (O), (Crimson Fancy), (941) 768-1119, no minimum order, catalog free.

Twombly Nursery (O), (203) 261-2133, call for minimum order, catalog $8.

Vintage Gardens (O), (707) 829-2035, no minimum order, catalog $5.

W. Atlee Burpee & Company (O), (Early Pick and Super Tasty varieties), (800) 888-1447, no minimum order, catalog free.

Wayside Gardens (O), 1 Garden Lane, Hodges, SC 29695-0001, (800) 845-1124, no minimum order, catalog free.

We-Du Nurseries (O), (704) 738-8300, after Oct. 1 dial (828) 738-8300, minimum shipping charge $6, catalog $2.

White Flower Farm (R), (800) 503-9624.

Wildflowers from Nature's Way (O), (515) 342-6246, $10 minimum order, catalog available.

Woodlanders, Inc. (O), 1128 Colleton Ave., Aiken, SC 29801, (803) 648-7522, $20 minimum order, catalog $2.

(M) Contact the manufacturer for a retail source near you. (O) Mail order; (R) Retail store. Unlisted items are one of a kind or unavailable.

Index

Plant Hardiness Zone Map

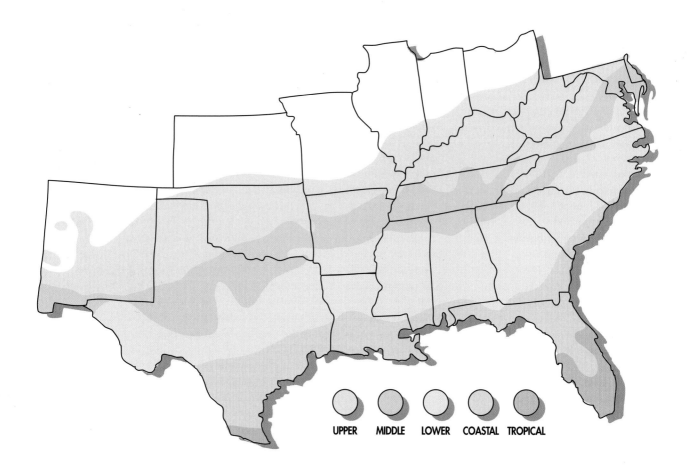

UPPER · MIDDLE · LOWER · COASTAL · TROPICAL

The United States Department of Agriculture has charted low temperatures throughout the country to determine the ranges of average low readings. The map above is based loosely on the USDA Plant Hardiness Zone Map, which was drawn from these findings. It does not take into account heat, soil, or moisture extremes and is intended as a guide, not a guarantee.

The southern regions of the United States that are mentioned in this book refer to the following:

Upper South: -10° to 0°F minimum
Middle South: 0° to 5°F minimum
Lower South: 5° to 15°F minimum
Coastal South: 15° to 25°F minimum
Tropical South: 25° to 40°F minimum